Praise for THE GLOBAL YOU

"If you are looking for a strategic, practical guide for preparing yourself to succeed in the global marketplace, relax, you've found it!"

—Dick Snyder, president and COO of ACO Inc, USA

"The fact that these ten strategies are based on research from global managers themselves builds a very solid foundation for the insights and practical advice offered in this book. Every manager has something worthwhile to learn in this study."

—Peter Hogarth, partner in JCA Coaching LLP, London

"An invaluable guide to the Global Village."

—Jeffrey Geri, author of *Culture Smart Israel*

"Embedding these ten practical strategies in your life will sustain your competitive edge in the global market."

—Olga Hafner, board director of
Meridian Wine Merchants, South Africa

"Susan Bloch and Philip Whiteley have done a remarkable job of assembling a set of strategies for preparing managers for the increasingly global organization and marketplace. The book is very thoughtful and very practical at the same time. The strategies suggested will be useful not just for building a global mindset but also for increasing managerial adaptability and mental flexibility in general. Indeed I would recommend the book for all managers, not just those assigned to global roles; for the latter I would say: Don't leave home without it."

—Gautam Ahuja, Harvey C. Fruehauf Professor of
Business Administration, Professor of Strategy, and
Chair of Strategy at the University of Michigan

THE
GLOBAL
YOU

SUSAN BLOCH & PHILIP WHITELEY

THE GLOBAL YOU

Ten strategies to operate
as an international business player

mc **Marshall Cavendish**
Business

Marshall Cavendish publishes an exciting range of books
on business, management and self-development.

If you would like to:
- Find out more about our titles
- Take advantage of our special offers
- Sign up to our e-newsletter

Please visit our
special website at: **www.business-bookshop.co.uk**

To the current as well as future Global Managers
who will bring economic stability, build cultural bridges,
and ensure peace for us all

CONTENTS

INTRODUCTION
WORKING IN THE BORDERLESS WORLD

When some of the world's largest financial institutions hit crisis in 2008, it was primarily national governments that rescued them. The governments used taxpayers' money to save "their" banks or "their" insurance companies—even when, as in the case of The Royal Bank of Scotland or AIG, the company's interests stretched right across the world.

Does this mean that for all the talk of a borderless world, globalization is only skin-deep, and that we still "really" live in a world of nation-states?

Your country is evidently still a powerful entity. It determines your passport, the language you speak, your right to work in specific parts of the world, and the taxes you pay. It may require you to engage in military service as well. In some countries, you even rely on it for health care and for an income in retirement. At an institutional level, then, the nation stands tall and proud as an influential player. Think of what soccer, cricket, or the Olympic Games do to national pride—or shame.

Yet, the nation-state is not dominant in all fields. Even in the example of the banking rescues, international groupings such as G8 and G20 are keen to set up international arrangements to prevent a recurrence of the crisis of 2008. Whether they will be able to move far enough, quickly enough, is a key test. The credit crisis gave finance ministers and prime ministers the fright of their lives; many are conscious that international companies in the private sector may one day generate liabilities that are beyond the scope of even the richest government to cope with. Given the level of indebtedness of many countries, the fate that befell Iceland—bankrupted by its international banks—could affect other, larger countries. Greece is still struggling for support from Germany and the European Union. Regulation and contingency planning are moving to the international sphere.

And in other sectors, the economic recession and crisis propelled greater, not less, international fusion. Airlines, for example, used to be characterized by "flag-carriers"—standard-bearers for the nation-states. The term is now an anachronism, as "flag-carriers" seek safety through mergers. British Airways and Spain's Iberia airline confirmed their tie-up in April 2010, in a culturally similar match to the take-over of the Abbey bank by Santander some years earlier. This is not only happening for airlines. In car manufacturing, Geely's purchase of Volvo means that the Chinese and Swedes will be working closely together, while in steel production, Tata's purchase of Corus will give the Indians, Dutch and British the same opportunity. Of course, there are countless other examples.

So even if you want to work for a "national" company, that option is rapidly disappearing. You are part of the global economy, and most probably a multi-cultural working experience, whether that was your career plan or not. And as currency fluctuations and national interest rates have an impact on import-export trading, some of the most powerful economic dynamics are now borderless.

But is *your* way of thinking, or your company's, truly borderless?

You really have no choice but to think about how you can become a global worker—and ultimately what we would term the Global You. It's not possible to shed your heritage—and we don't recommend that. It's also not possible to absorb all cultures and worldviews. But it *is* possible to begin to perceive the world from different standpoints and to become more aware of your own culture—its strengths and limitations—and to learn of the merits of others.

A trend that we have observed over the years is the growth of migration—often of middle-class professionals, not solely people trying to escape poverty. There are more people becoming "global" in outlook, both by accident and design.

Inventions to enable fast travel between continents and instant communication through the internet are occurring more rapidly than our ability to comprehend the "new" cultures and ways of working that we thereby come into contact with. We, who form the "human internet," need to learn how to listen to one another, solve problems and make decisions quickly—in other parts of the world, which we might not really understand. We still remain the mule, struggling, somewhat breathlessly, to catch up with the technological bullet train.

There is a tendency in business to think that international working is mostly about logistics. However, our experience, together with our collated research data, shows that it's a much more multi-dimensional challenge. It's often the building of relationships and the creating of mutual understanding, rather than the technical skills, that represent the biggest challenge. Perhaps if Tony Hayward, BP's CEO, had taken the time and trouble to connect with folk on the ground as soon as oil leaked into the Gulf, both he and BP would be in a better place?

To operate on the global stage, it is important to be curious, adaptable, and comfortable with uncertainty and ambiguity. Often global working means reconciling apparent opposites: understanding that the economy is both national and global; accepting that people are the same, but different; respecting other cultures while staying true to our values; seeking alignment of a working team while tolerating dissent; asserting ourselves as individuals while promoting teamwork; using virtual communications while deepening real relationships; recognising that the hardship of learning new languages brings the comfort of multi-cultural savvy. Once you learn to handle the ambiguity of these seemingly irreconcilable terms—and indeed to marry them—you will be well on your way to becoming the Global You.

This may sound daunting, but we've sought to make the quest to become the Global You as practical as possible. When you visit an unfamiliar country, it's helpful to take a travel guide with you. Our aim here is to create a travel guide to that unknown country called "borderless working."

Our observations and advice are based on research, discussions, interviews, coaching and personal experience. We come from different cultures and countries, and between us we have lived and worked in every continent except Antarctica. In addition, we have carried out surveys of over 700 hundred workers, and interviews with dozens more. Most operate in a global context—about 20 per cent have not had global experience—and have positive tales to tell about working and thriving in complex, international teams. All this data has been calibrated and distilled into ten clear strategies:

1. **Think global.** Are you up to date on the socio-economic and political climates in the countries you are doing business with? When you wake up in the morning, are you reading the local or international news? Are you watching some of the international news channels? Have you studied the governance and legal complexities of the companies you plan to do business with? Are you constantly developing that "borderless" mindset so essential for a global worldview?

2. **Learn to work in a multi-cultural context.** Study the "Dos and Don'ts" of different cultures, countries and religions. You have to be able to engage with people from anywhere and everywhere, while blocking prejudices and stereotypes about religions and cultures unconsciously imbibed over the years.

3. **Travel whenever you can—for fun or for work.** And when you do, take the time to get on a local bus or train, and mix with the locals, rather than stay in your "Western-style" hotel, disengaged from the local population. Immersing yourself in another culture is the best way to come to understanding it. Take an assignment in another country;

attend conferences; visit business sites. For those who can't get away, there are still ways to reach out and connect internationally.

4. **Learn a language.** Learning a new language is not just about the technical knowledge of vocabulary and grammar. It encompasses learning a different worldview, based on the distinct features of the language in question—terms that have no direct equivalent; other words that appear to be similar, but actually mean something subtly different. This allows the Global You to overcome the most common frustration of global working: communication difficulties. And there are many hidden advantages as well.

5. **Learn to learn out of the classroom.** Learn via "webinars" (web-based seminars), podcasts, beamed lectures, video-conferences (VCs), mobile-enabled learning (MEL), and even gaming. In the global world, you will also have to learn to be comfortable with ambiguities, to consider the "big picture," and to assimilate rapidly changing contexts.

6. **Go virtual while staying real.** Constantly update your multimedia skills; get comfortable with virtual forms of communication. Choose the best medium. For some purposes, video conferencing is perfect; for others telephone is better; and sometimes it's necessary to meet in person.

New technology is only a means to an end; it's all about communication. The medium has to suit the message.

7. **Treat multi-cultural teamwork as a core skill.** Companies often have to have a global reach to be viable— this means working in international teams with members from different cultures. These differences can be productive: the best solutions develop from a healthy debate over diverse ideas; so learn to ask the right questions and listen to the answers.

8. **Build your personal network.** Structures are often fluid. You may be working in a matrix structure, and managing people who do not report to you. Operating globally is about managing relationships, not business structures. It helps to draw a map of your key colleagues, customers and vendors: Who is really important? Are they the people you spend most time talking to and engaging with? In a smaller business, or as a sole trader, these networks become even more critical.

9. **Raise your global profile.** Web 2.0 offers opportunities for promoting your career profile, being an online publisher, and creating an international network—which help with identifying new customers and markets, connecting with peers and friends and maximizing learning opportunities.

10. **Manage your time across time zones.** You might often have to start your day early, or end late, to connect with colleagues, customers or vendors who are in different time zones. Learn how to fit work into odd pockets of time, stave off jet lag, and have the awareness of world time at your fingertips.

Chapter by chapter, these ten strategies will be examined in turn. Preparation, planning and practice are the "3 Ps" that will guarantee successful implementation of these strategies.

1 THINK GLOBAL

Sunil Gupta started the day early in New York, having set his alarm clock (MADE IN JAPAN) for 6 a.m. While his coffee-pot (MADE IN CHINA) was perking, he shaved with his electric razor (MADE IN KOREA). He put on a shirt (MADE IN MYANMAR), a suit (MADE IN SINGAPORE), a tie (MADE IN THAILAND) and shoes (MADE IN CHINA, DESIGNED IN ITALY). He fried an egg in his new electric skillet (MADE IN INDIA). After setting his watch (MADE IN TAIWAN) to the radio (MADE IN INDIA), he got in his car (MADE IN GERMANY), and en route to work, topped up the tank with gasolene (FROM SAUDI ARABIA). At the office he checked his email on his PC (MADE IN KOREA), and took a call on his mobile (MADE IN CHINA), running on the latest software (DESIGNED IN THE USA).

"It's very hard these days to be a truly domestic company," observes Andrew Sherman, adjunct professor in the MBA and Executive MBA programmes at the University of Maryland, USA, in an interview with the business website, portfolio.com. He adds: "Even your local restaurant down the street may be buying some of its ingredients or supplies from abroad. If you're a regional company, say in the south-eastern United States, there's still a lot of the country you've not penetrated. But at some point you're going to get contacted by a customer or vendor in another country, or you're going to have an interest in a foreign market. It may be Canada, the Caymans, or Latin America."

Even if you have never so much as left the state you are in, you are still plugged into a global economy. Indeed, you might not realize it, but you *depend* upon it—for the very basics of life, like food. This is true even for countries where the staple food is one of its main agricultural products. In October 2009, Bloomberg reported: "Rice futures surged to a nine-month high in Chicago after the Philippines, the world's biggest importer, said it may boost overseas purchases because storms have damaged the domestic crop."

A global state of mind

If you are reading this book, you know the importance of this. You may be engaged globally, as a "borderless" worker as well as consumer. You may be working in a country different from the one you grew up in. You may also have discovered that for all our interconnectedness through trade, people from different parts of the world still have sharply different cultural upbringings and outlooks. There are cultural differences that can affect us in our work, and these should not and cannot be ignored.

Prior to these challenges of interacting globally, however, there's an even more basic one: How do we see *ourselves*, our company, our country of birth, and their respective roles in the world? Do we think locally, or globally? Do we concern ourselves primarily with the consumers, laws and politics of one nation or state, or have we learned to think across borders, simultaneously?

The purpose of this book is to encourage a more global worldview, one that will equip you to make the most of advantages in the interconnected economy. This is relevant to you in many ways:

- You never know when you might be working abroad, either living there or just doing short stints of business.

- You may suddenly find yourself in a multi-cultural, borderless company, for example through a cross-border merger.

- Your customers may be local right now, but who knows when they will be in another country?

- The goods and services you are selling may depend partly or wholly on vendors or partners in another country. Think, for example, of who you are talking to when you call your bank. It could be a call centre in Ireland, Poland, South Africa or India. Or it could still be local.

Having a global mindset, acknowledging global behaviours, and developing global traits—cultivating, in other words, the Global You—are essentials for remaining highly employable. What could be more important, in times of economic uncertainty, than to ensure that companies will always want to work with or for you?

It's not necessary for the Global You to have equal knowledge of, or give equal attention to, all countries of the world. What's important is to understand different worldviews, and to appreciate a multi-polar view of the world. You never know when your knowledge, attitude and traits will be called upon, for deployment on the international stage.

No such thing as the centre of the world

In 1988 the *National Geographic* asked 3,800 children from 49 countries to each draw a map of the world. All of them—including the African and Asian children—drew Europe in the centre of their map.

What this reflected was the worldwide influence of a very culturally specific view of the world—that of 16th-century European Imperialism—as immortalized in the Mercator projection, surely the most commonly viewed map of the world.

Maps are never neutral. The Mercator projection, from the 16th century, places Europe at the centre; but then, it was designed by a European cartographer for European seafarers. It used fidelity of the angles, making countries look larger the nearer they were to the poles. It reflects the dominance of European economic power in the 16th to 20th centuries. Later versions increased the distortion, by subtly moving the Equator below the half-way mark, so that the Northern Hemisphere took up around two-thirds of the map's area. Visitors from Europe to, say, South America can be amazed at the distances involved. The Paraguay River, which looks modest on a conventional map, is actually part of one of the largest river systems in the world. Travelling along it, starting from Asunción in Paraguay—which though a thousand miles inland has a deep-water harbour—upstream to the Pantanal in Brazil, takes no less than four days.

In a similar way, British Imperial maps were deliberately distorted to make the Northern Hemisphere look larger than the Southern (and, of course, had a quarter of the world's land masses painted pink for "Empire"). Greenland appeared to be bigger than Brazil, whereas in fact it is about a quarter of the size. The British Isles looked like a medium-sized archipelago near the centre of the world, not the small set of islands near one of the poles that they actually are.

These old, Europe-based maps, if represented in three dimensions, would be like an inverted pear: a bulbous, outsized Northern Hemisphere, and a shrunken, tapered Southern Hemisphere. They are metaphors for the ways in which people perceive the world in terms of the importance of different regions— in this case with Europe occupying prime position.

But is this European dominance coming to an end? In March 2010, the Spanish newspaper *El Pais* ran an article headed "Europe is wiped from the map." It recalled the *National Geographic* survey, and reported how "cartograms" and the evolving world order are changing the actual and imaginary maps with which we perceive the world. (For example, on websites such as worldmapper.org, the territories of the world can be *resized* according to various parameters—anything from housing prices, women's income, or fuel consumption to the number of aircraft departures, hospital beds, cellular subscribers.)

The article also drew attention to the economic and demographic projections indicating that the USA, China, Brazil and India are likely to be the dominant powers in the coming century. It concluded by asking whether, by the year 2050, "if *National Geographic* repeated the experiment, European children would draw China and the USA in the centre and relegate Europe to the extreme west of the world map" ("Europa se borra del mapa," *El Pais*, 20 March 2010).

And as for the British Imperial worldview, there's now a neat wall map you can buy that inverts the most common image of the world. It features the Southern Hemisphere at the top, with New Zealand placed near the centre. It's titled "No Longer Down Under."

It is impossible to be certain where the future centres of economic power will be. But one thing is clear: there is no longer—if there ever was—a single most important centre of the world. This is a particularly important insight if you live in a large, "happening" place like New York, Shanghai, Berlin, Rio de Janeiro, Mumbai or London. It can appear as if it is the centre of all things important, but in a multi-polar world, this is an illusion.

What does your map look like?

Each of us probably has our own world map embedded in our subconscious; it might be similar to the familiar Europe-centred one—or very different. So a useful exercise to begin "thinking globally" is to ask yourself: *What shape is 'my' map?*

The cultural influences we have absorbed since childhood will have exaggerated or minimized the importance of certain regions, distorting their true weighting. Even apparently geographically defined terms can mean different things to different people, depending on upbringing. Given that two of the ambiguous or contentious terms are "America" and "China," this is no small matter.

Added to our perceptions of size and influence, we will have notions of the friendliness or hostility of other nations, regions or groups, based on the history of the culture we grew up in. These can be very strong. For example, if you are from the USA and aged under 40, what was the image of Iran that you were raised with, given the seismic impact of the 1979 revolution and the aftermath? And, of course, vice versa if you are from Iran.

We cannot eradicate the influence of these subconscious perceptions, but by making them conscious, we will arrive at a more balanced view. This is a useful exercise to practise as part of the process of becoming a global worker.

So, what does your map look like? Is it still the one from your childhood? Does that still guide your view of the world? Are there serious distortions in it that deserve to be challenged? What are the narratives that lie behind these images? Who are the heroes? Who are the villains?

Our local neighbourhood, company and government dominate our consciousness. Their affairs seem important. And indeed they are, in context. But they may be of little consequence in global terms. Thinking globally involves understanding different worldviews—something that helps us "Think Global." But an even more basic requirement is gaining a sense of perspective, an acknowledgement of the sheer size, as well as diversity, of the growing human population.

Where do you get your information?

Images and stories, imbibed in our younger years, can be either reinforced or challenged by the messages we receive daily. This makes our sources of information one of the key matters to focus

EXERCISE
TAKE A GLOBE AND SPIN IT ROUND

Here's an idea if you've lived mostly in one country or region. Take a globe, and spin it around so that you are looking at it from an unfamiliar angle. (You could use Google Maps, but representation on a flat screen involves distortion, so an old-fashioned globe is best.)

Look at the world from that unfamiliar angle for a few minutes. Does it look different? Does your sense of a focal point "feel" different? Perhaps you are surprised at how big Indonesia is. Or Mexico. Perhaps "your" part of the world, which you had tacitly assumed to be at the hub of all matters important, now looks like a rather distant little corner. It hasn't, of course, suddenly become less important; what's changed is your awareness of a larger, multi-polar world, with hundreds of markets and thousands of different worldviews.

Now, choose five countries besides your own that you think you know best, and write down the following:

- Who is the prime minister or president?
- What is the main language spoken there? What other languages do locals speak?
- What religions do they practise?
- What are the most important products or services that are available there? (For example, for Switzerland it could be banking and tourism.)

continued >>>

- What is the overall population?
- Have you ever met or worked with anyone from that country?

This exercise is particularly valuable for those who live in larger economies, where the domestic economy looms large; but even if you have travelled or worked overseas considerably, it's still a useful exercise to carry out from time to time.

on when switching to thinking globally. When watching, reading or listening to the news, remember to include some of the international news channels, rather than rely on only local, domestic channels, papers or websites. It pays to study the governance, history and legal complexities of the companies you plan to do business with and the countries they are in. If you are based on the US East Coast, supplement your usual news from the *New York Times*, Bloomberg News channel, CNN and Fox by reading the *International Herald Tribune*, and *The Economist*, the *Times of India*, or listening to the BBC World Service or Al-Jazeera. Most of this is available online. This is the news-gathering equivalent of tipping up the globe and looking at the world from a new vantage point. It could remind you that the rest of the world doesn't care about US health care reform unless its highly charged politics affect the standing of President Obama. Yet it's an issue that every American is deeply concerned about.

If you rely primarily on news media from your home country to inform yourself on world events, on the basis that it has a large and well-written foreign news section, this still leaves significant gaps in your knowledge. In most countries, the overseas news coverage reflects the historic patterns of trade of that nation, and the location of the diaspora of its natives. So the foreign news section will probably not offer a balanced overview of world affairs.

For example, the political upheavals of Peru in recent decades were given far more coverage in *El Pais* of Madrid, than in *The Times* of London. (*The Times* gives priority to events of similar magnitude that occur in South Africa, Australia, Zimbabwe or India—countries previously or still part of the Commonwealth.) By extension, all the countries of the Spanish-speaking world can be thought of as constituting one economic region, even though they span different continents, such is the depth and extent of trade, investment and migration between them. Consequently, they are likely to pay more attention in their media to one another's affairs than to those of the non-Spanish-speaking world.

Breaking out of the national silo

Given that globalization has been around for a long time—since the Harappan civilization (4000 BC), through the Greeks and Romans (1000 BC), to the great explorations from the 1400s on—it is surprising to find out the extent to which business leaders are still struggling with the challenge of a global orientation, especially now that technology enables them to communicate almost anywhere and anytime.

This struggle reflects sheer global diversity and the difficulty of acknowledging and engaging with different worldviews. Moreover, the universal terms of reference of business—the balance sheet, the commonality of products, especially computer-based ones—give an illusion of universality to the international economy, leaving you skating on the surface.

The top teams of many companies are often still dominated by male nationals of that company's country of origin or location of headquarters—despite the fact that most of the manufacturing or sales and marketing of its products take place in other countries or continents. Asian examples are Reliance, Toyota, Wipro and Infosys; Western ones would be Coca-Cola, HSBC, Amex, Unilever, Shell and so on. Many of these, and other companies, are seeking, yet still struggling, to ensure diversity at the top. There is a surprising degree of inertia, even today.

The struggle faced by global leaders is, first of all, the result of practical matters of communication, problems with language, and time differences. Strange as it may seem, even though most people speak English, there are many phrases that get "lost in translation," leaving people confused and often upset. Time differences are often ignored, so that conference calls are organized to suit corporate leaders, not even bothering to think that it may be midnight for other team members.

Cultural differences present an equally tough challenge. A large percentage of leaders are relatively unknowledgeable about those parts of the world where they are doing business—about their customs, etiquette, and socio-political issues. Some are quite insular. In this situation, it is a common default mode for leaders to assume that people think like they do—or that they ought to. And to be irritated when they find that often they don't.

All [my company's] data backup work was outsourced to a company in India, in Ahmedabad. I thought it would work like clockwork. After about six months I thought it would be good to go out and meet them. To start off, I hadn't realized how far Ahmedabad was from Mumbai and that it was another flight from there. When I did finally visit India and the offices, I felt completely overwhelmed as to how things worked over there. I wished I had taken the time to read up about the country, even very basic stuff. Firstly, the office only opened at 10 in the morning, and everyone seemed to be talking non-stop all the time on their mobile phones. They were not switched off during meetings, which initially I found extremely rude, but everyone there does it. Even though the team there appeared very warm and welcoming, everything, even having a "boy" to do the photocopying, felt so strange.

I realized I should have made the visit months earlier. This was more than us just dumping work on them, but required collaboration and communication. Yet it was only months later over dinner, that I came to realize that they too had a worldview of the USA, especially with regard to America's policy towards Pakistan. They didn't love America as I thought they would. I should have realized that almost a year earlier, but it had not even entered my head.

—Chief Administrator of a legal firm based in Chicago:

Anyone who has overseen an international outsourcing deal will tell you that transaction cost quite quickly becomes a minor matter compared with the challenges of management and cultural understanding.

Overcoming resistance to globalization

Globalization is often politically controversial. Outsourcing projects are frequently denounced as cynical exercises in cutting transaction costs (and of course there is often much justice in this view); employing "foreigners" rather than locals is regularly debated in the press and in parliaments. Such noises have increased since the global economic downturn began in 2008, and protectionist sympathies have come increasingly to the fore.

People, no matter how well-educated or widely-travelled, still seem to be more comfortable with their own kind, and distrustful of foreigners. You will still come across the view that "locals" are considered not well-educated enough, or unambitious, or lazy, and therefore non-promotable.

Just about all of the business leaders whom we have spoken with acknowledge that this challenge of overcoming the national silo needs to be addressed. Almost all struggle with it despite the negative impact on business performance.

This can only be overcome by "thinking globally"—by taking time to develop yourself, by seizing opportunities in international working, and by identifying tangible benefits for individuals, teams and businesses. It is no use putting your head in the sand, in the hope it will all go away. The starting point is "being global," and recognizing that unless acknowledged and addressed, the challenge of thinking and working globally will eventually snowball.

International working can be rewarding, even if it is difficult. Many global workers have had very positive experiences. Going global can in fact even be liberating. You will find that there can actually be more opportunities and fewer barriers working internationally than working in the country of your upbringing, where your religious or class background can cause you to suffer discrimination. Often just your name, or where you went to school, becomes an automatic barrier in your home country—but abroad may be ignored.

EXERCISE
PRACTISE YOUR GLOBAL THINKING

Take a minute to think about the products and services that your business has for sale. Then think about your customers. Are they all local? Are some from other parts of the country or even from another country? Then ask yourself how much you know about the towns, states, or countries they live in. Set yourself this quiz:

- If they live in another town, how big is it and what is the ethnic mix or religious mix?
- If it is another country, how many people live there? What kind of food do they eat? What is the weather like compared to your own weather now?

continued >>>

- What languages do they speak? Are you able to speak any of those languages?
- How often do you connect with people from that town/country? Are they social or business contacts?
- Have you ever visited that particular location? Was it for business or pleasure?

Write down everything you know about that area, and then compare it with the information on *Lonely Planet*, or *Time Out*, or Wikipedia. You might even find an appropriate travel programme to download or view on TV.

Now think about your vendors and suppliers. Where do they come from? Then ask yourself the same set of questions that you just asked about your customers.

Do this for each country or zone that your customers and vendors originate from. Do the same for your colleagues and team members, your friends and family. You will be surprised to learn how many colleagues and friends you have in so many different places. Try to visit them— either for work or fun.

Now when you read a newspaper or article, keep a "hook out" for the locations you have listed. Keep your antennae alert for news items and mentions of those places to which you are connected. Try to build up a picture of what it's like to live there; what the recent history might be; what people are concerned about.

Business is not just the balance sheet

This deeper knowledge of the world's regions is a business concern, not just a matter of geographic curiosity. As noted, decisions on acquisitions, outsourcing, joint ventures and so on are often made on the two-dimensional criteria of the balance sheet, market share and growth opportunities. Getting value from them typically requires a three-dimensional perspective that encompasses deep knowledge about the people living and working there.

It's a good idea, therefore, to add societal as well as local-management due diligence to the traditional analyses based on markets and finance. Take this testimony from the Head of Operations of a UK cosmetics company, who was surprised at the differences over just a narrow stretch of sea:

> We acquired a company in France, and didn't realize how little most of us knew about life over there. This despite the fact that quite a few of us had been on holiday to Paris or Provence. We had little understanding of the political scene, and got completely ambushed by the unions. Before we knew what had happened we had a strike looming. We, the management, had little general understanding of how strong the unions were. To top it all we hadn't acknowledged how differently French women and girls used cosmetics compared to their British counterparts. Different shades, different combinations, and more emphasis on the "eyes."

The particular trap here lies in assuming that a place or culture nearby is going to be very similar. If you're based in California and you're setting up in China, cultural differences should loom large in your consciousness. What's less obvious, as this British manager found, is that a UK company in France, or an Italian company in Austria, or a Thai company in Cambodia, may have very steep learning curves. Even *within* countries there can be cultural differences. Many people from north-eastern states in the USA might feel more at home in Italy or France—especially if they have ancestry in those countries and enjoy regular visits to family there—than they would in rural parts of southern states like Georgia, or South Carolina. Economics on its own is not enough.

Think future, study history

It helps to know at least a little of the history of a region you are visiting, working in, or doing business with. This enables you to appreciate that what happened in the past was never inevitable. Understanding this—and understanding how seismic shifts in markets, balances of political power, popular tastes and strength of empires can happen with rapidity and unpredictability—helps prepare you for the future. This is a delicious "paradox": understanding the past as a route to becoming more adaptable, global and forward-thinking.

Don't forget history.

The past kept in mind is a guide to the future.

—Sign in the Memorial to the Nanjing Massacre,
Nanjing, China; in English, Chinese, Japanese

The micro-trend that suddenly becomes big; Google of a decade ago; Indian software of 20 years ago; a scarcely noticed announcement by Mikhail Gorbachev in mid-1989 that he wouldn't send the tanks in to stop people leaving Eastern Europe. These are all reminders that it's worth monitoring the trends in the political and commercial landscape. The balance of power between countries, or companies, can change with remarkable speed.

Moreover, history keeps raising its ugly head in the contemporary world, even where it seems to be dead and buried. Where it does, there are often different narratives emerging in different countries and regions—or even within countries. There are also, often, pragmatic groups of people who challenge the more divisive and sectarian movements.

Belgium presents a useful illustration of this, with lessons for multicultural countries, and merged companies, everywhere. There are two regions, two languages, and three dominant narratives. The future of the nation depends on which one wins. Since the elections of June 2010, there has been a rise in support for the richer, Dutch-speaking Flanders to become independent; the narrative is that this region should not have to subsidize the French-speaking Wallonia in the south. Many in the Francophone region, however, argue that to keep the nation together, the north should show "solidarity," that it's only natural that a richer region support a poorer one in rough times, as part of the unofficial contract that keeps a nation together. In the middle are bilingual people who favour a deeper dialogue to resolve these problems—to help ensure that solidarity exists, but also that it is not abused and does not become dependence.

A nice article in *Le Monde* (27 July 2010) profiled four young female friends from both sides of the language divide, living together and learning each other's languages. In the interview, the four blamed male politicians for fanning the flames of regional envy and separatism. One of them, Noemie, commented:

> *Dutch speakers or Francophones... we can communicate perfectly well, as long as each side makes an effort. It is enough to mix with each other. Older people do not do so, but the younger generation is more open.*

These individuals were not prepared to let the separatist narratives of older politicians guide their lives and career choices. Which narrative will win? Independence for the north, welfare for the south, or a bilingual reconciliation?

My first stint working in Poland was bound to be uncomfortable, given that I am of Jewish descent. The holocaust still loomed large, given that my wife's father had perished in a concentration camp there. This discomfort was probably apparent, as the first thing my regional manager told me over dinner was that his father had been shot by the Gestapo for being a resistance fighter. I had no idea that any non-Jews had been active in the resistance in Krakow, and felt my face burn with embarrassment.

—South African operations manager
in an international brewery company

The person is not the country

A similar situation can been seen in the case of Daniel Barenboim, the celebrated conductor. Barenboim, who holds Argentinian, Israeli and Spanish citizenship, in 1999 co-founded the West-Eastern Divan, an orchestra that brings together musicians from all over the Middle East—Israeli, Palestinian, Egyptian, Iranian, Jordanian, Lebanese, and Syrian—in an effort to bring about intercultural understanding in this region fraught with tensions. This is a clear demonstration that political narratives can be consciously resisted and challenged by individuals—*the person is not the country.*

News headlines inevitably focus on the big conflicts. Underneath, there are often thousands of pragmatic people forming their own views, and their own relationships, in directions very different from that of the business and political leaders of "their" country.

News is published based on its impact; there is no requirement to give a balanced view. Recurring stories, especially negative stories, thus create an impression of a country that can be quite misleading. So countries like Colombia, Congo, Iran and Afghanistan have an "image" in the Western world that is not very favourable.

One of the recurring problems, therefore, that we have come across in international working, is the unconsciously patronizing attitude that managers from the richer countries can have towards people from developing countries—based on assumptions that people in poorer countries are backward, underdeveloped, less well-educated, or less well-organized. Very often, levels of education and understanding, and forms of organization, are as high or higher in poorer countries; but they seem so different.

Yet most people within these countries simply want to have a good job, or build a good business, and to do well for their families. In fact, a major survey of people all over the world, carried out by the opinion survey specialist Gallup in 2007, found that, for all the bewildering array of diverse cultures across the world, there is a common desire in the hearts and minds of people across all countries: "I want a good job." Researchers found this recurring as a dominant desire, as they put it, "in Khartoum, Tehran, Berlin, Lima, Los Angeles, Baghdad, Kolkata or Istanbul."

So, while we are all different, at the core we are all the same.

Thinking globally—an ongoing discipline

It is, of course, impossible to get under the skin of all cultures and worldviews within the scope of a single life. Thinking globally isn't a utopian vision of trying to absorb every single culture. It's better to think of it as a process: a way of orientating yourself towards considering all parts of the world as potential markets, and potential places to work, relocate or do business. It also means understanding that the many different worldviews around the world can be sharply different, and that they are not necessarily better or worse than your own—just different. Importantly, recognize your own prejudices. Stand back, reflect and take a more impartial view.

This first strategy—of thinking global—can only really be achieved by attending to the second strategy—of gaining an understanding of different places and cultures, as we'll show you in the next chapter. Learning about a different culture is an endless educational challenge in itself.

THINKING GLOBALLY IN A BORDERLESS WAY

- Learn to look at the world from the opposite hemisphere. Think not only about your views on different cultures, food, and religions, but importantly, others' views about yours.

- Gather news about the world from international sources. Read the *Economist*, *McKinsey Quarterly*, *Newsweek* and *National Geographic*, as well as the daily papers of various regions, e.g. *The Bangkok Times*, *The Financial Times*, *The New York Times*, *The Times of India*, etc.

- Learn and understand news about your company from diverse sources within the organization.

- Build up a sense of perspective of the scale of different regions. Is your new call centre geographically close to the capital, or a thousand miles away, for example? Map out distances from major cities, and from your own home base.

- Remember that there are sharp cultural differences between neighbouring countries, and even between different states within the same country. Take time to table them, acknowledge them, and accept them.

- Thinking globally is a continuous process. Plan how you are going to keep up to date with those areas with which you are most likely to be connected—for example by using Google Alerts, or RSS feeds.

2 LEARN TO WORK IN A MULTI-CULTURAL CONTEXT

On a recent business trip to Turkey, William F., CFO of a global company, managed to have an evening off, and took a boat trip down the Bosporus. There was a group of Chinese tourists on board and he was keen to connect with them, as China was seen as a key new market for them. This proved to be near impossible, as none of them spoke any English except for the rather glamorous tour guide. After a rather serious conversation with her, she suddenly asked him if she could sing him a Chinese song. A polite yes, and a melodic song was sung. As William was nervous that she was romancing him, he made a hasty exit when the boat docked. Incident soon forgotten. Six months later, after frenzied negotiations with his Shanghai counterpart were finally concluded, William, on the way to the airport, was surprised to hear the same question: "Would you like to hear a Chinese song?" It was only months later he came to learn that this offer was a sign of respect and courtesy.

Questions of culture

Different rituals and behaviours from different countries and cultures are often very confusing, and sometimes misinterpreted. When we compare people across the globe, we are at the same time very similar, yet very different. We all experience happiness, anger, jealousy, joy and grief. Yet we express ourselves and behave in very different ways. Just a quick look across continents highlights how Americans, Chinese, Lithuanians, New Zealanders and Indians are worlds apart in every respect: history, culture, religion, language, geography and eating habits. How many of you have experienced a wedding in India, or a funeral in Soweto, whether personally or through some media? And when we go deeper into some individual countries, we find that the people in South Africa, for example, or Belgium, are like antipodes contained within the borders of a single country.

When travelling to smaller towns and cities, like Jharkhand in India, which see few foreign visitors, the locals, especially children, love to connect and talk. "What is your name, where are you from, do you like our food?" or "Can we have a photo with you?" are typical conversation-starters. Locals are often eager to ask further questions like "Is everyone very rich in London?" or "Will America bomb Iran?" And importantly, no matter what their views, everyone speaks about international trade links. "Our markets are full of toys from China, but we run all the call centres for the banks in the UK" is frequently heard in India.

Such comments reveal the sheer complexity of the modern and historical global landscape. For another example, consider that while on the one hand, many Jews have deep-seated nightmares about the Holocaust, yet Israel and Germany conduct high levels of trade between them. Similarly, Japan will never forget the atom bombs on Hiroshima and Nagasaki, nor the Americans the attack on Pearl Harbour; but think for a minute about the number of Japanese cars on the roads in the US, and the number of American companies, such as Walmart, McDonalds and KFC, in Japan. No wonder conflicting emotions and ideas can exist in the mind of one single manager.

Little signals: Big messages

In the USA or UK, if a driver flashes his car lights at you, it means "Please go ahead and cross the road." In India, it means "Watch out, I am not going to slow down, so get out of the way... fast."

This observation, by a participant in a workshop run by an Indian company in early 2010, serves as useful traffic advice in itself, but also as a neat illustration of human behaviour that has radically different local interpretations. (As an aside, it's worth pointing out that British drivers flashing their lights as a friendly invitation are acting *against* their own country's Highway Code, which insists that such use of lights should be a warning. So a well-prepared Indian visitor who had taken the trouble to learn the local laws would be doubly surprised. This British habit has grown up entirely informally, like most local customs and habits.)

Bridging cultural gaps

In Chapter 1 you tipped up the globe and looked at the world from a new geographical angle. Now it is time to add another dimension: a fresh *cultural* vantage point. In addition to reading or watching media from different regions, why not read unfamiliar sections of the newspaper? If you normally confine yourself to the politics and business sections, read the theatre reviews. If you're a sports devotee, read the poetry; if you're an aficionado of the fine arts, read the sports section. Listen to a talk by a representative of a political party you normally oppose, and give him a fair hearing. If you don't care for country-and-western music, or African-Caribbean, or opera, give it a listen; try to get a feel for what engages others in the music.

The best way of learning about a region or a country may be by reading a novel, rather than non-fiction; try *The Plague*, by Albert Camus, for France; or *The Long Song*, by Andrea Levy, for Jamaica; or *The House of the Spirits*, by Isabel Allende, for Chile. Rituals around food and dining, too, can be a useful insight into another culture—and worth learning about, to avoid making faux pas.

These "excursions" out of your usual interest areas will give you a continuing education in the multiple worldviews and narratives of the diverse human population, equipping you for the challenge of working in multi-national teams.

Cross-cultural empathy, like other human skills, benefits from exercise. It's not easy when you yourself have had to confront discrimination and prejudice. Chuck Maxwell, a management consultant based in Atlanta, Georgia, USA, adds:

> I am labeled "African-American," which carries a lot of unwanted and unnecessary baggage. I also grew up in the southern United States, which is well-known for the biases toward people of color. However, I understand the uneducated reactions, and then proceed forward to complete the tasks at hand using my skills. I also turn on the charm, talk to people so that I am not "different" from them. Once they learn of my diversity and social/global awareness, the workplace becomes a pleasant place to be.

Cultural differences can be bridged via shared concerns. In researching *How to Manage in a Flat World*, it was clear that diversity comes in many dimensions: there can be easier bonding between, for example, software engineers from five different continents, than between different professional groupings of the same nationality. This highlights the importance of having common interests or expertise. Just watch a group of women—from anywhere—chatting away. They always seem to connect easily over career opportunities and the complexities of balancing work and home priorities.

It may be difficult to swallow

In the 6 Apr 2010 edition of *The Economist*, the following appeared:

> *Natto, a food that has achieved infamy among Japan's foreign residents. With lacings of British understatement, the BBC recently described it as "a fermented soy bean dish that many consider an acquired taste." This is too kind. Quietly offensive, its whiff recalls a long-neglected, moulding food scrap. Indeed, that is pretty much what it is. Be this as it may, natto is the food with which, sooner or later, the foreign visitor is likely to have to deal. The natto challenge usually occurs once the sake is flowing. Socializing between colleagues and with clients is an integral part of doing business in Japan: salarymen boast that in Japan business is done by "nomunication," a compound (of the punning type beloved by Japanese) of "nomu" (to drink) and "communication." And in Japan it is a rule that alcohol should be accompanied by food of some description. In circumstances such as these your straight-laced [sic] day-time interlocutor can turn into a gleeful tormenter—leaning across the table to goad you with the suspect morsel: "Try this. Foreigners can't eat it, you know." All eyes*

will fall upon you as you sit awkwardly on the floor. Your room for manoeuvre is limited: it is poor form to refuse food in Japan.

It is not uncommon for travellers to search out familiar food whichever country they find themselves in, and stick to restaurants in 5-star hotels which cater to any needs. If that suits you it is fine. Be careful though if you are lunching in the staff canteen, or invited to someone's home. As with natto, food can make or break a relationship.

Same aims, different emphasis

Differences in interpersonal relations also exist. In Latin America, it is customary for people to express warm emotions and convey excitement, even quite early in a business relationship, whereas in Northern Europe this may be disapproved of, and even considered a symptom of immaturity. North America probably lies somewhere in between those two extremes.

An example of a central corporate initiative not translating well to diverse locations occurred at an international hotel chain a few years ago. A very "American" edict on "How to smile at guests" was sent out from Boston to all its global offices, but was not always interpreted or enacted locally in the way envisaged. For example, in Turkey, where you don't have to "train" people to smile at guests, the staff thought this was very stupid, and ridiculed it. In Britain the sense of forced jollity made some people feel embarrassed, and felt out of place.

If you think you can get by just carrying on the way you usually do in your home country, please read this vignette:

I lived [in China] in the mid-1980s while I was working as a journalist. Throughout that period, every time something of consequence occurred there would be a three-day gestation period before all of the pieces fell together and I understood what actually had happened. Back then, I blamed this time lag on cultural differences. In retrospect, it also involved the vast chasm between someone raised in a free society and those used to a totalitarian one.

One summer afternoon in 1985, posters went up in my neighborhood announcing a "friendly swimming competition." There were never enough opportunities to really mix with my Chinese neighbors: We would smile at each other and exchange greetings, but it rarely went beyond that. So I accepted any chance that came along.

Unlike most Western journalists in China at that time, I lived in a Chinese neighborhood in a typical Chinese apartment. Granted, the seven other British and American families in the unit were all sequestered together in one section of the building with our own entrance. But everyone around us was Chinese, which made us feel like we actually lived in China.

When the day of the swimming competition arrived one warm Sunday in July, I walked over to the local pool with all of my neighbors. I remember it as one of the more pleasant afternoons that summer, with a lot of laughing and kidding around.

I have never been much of an athlete, but I was on the swim team in high school so I thought there was a chance I might not embarrass myself. I had signed up for three events and to my surprise I managed to win all three races. Prizes were even given out, which I promptly passed on to my Chinese friends. I remember one was a bottle of perfume.

But over the next two weeks, I noticed something that should have registered with me immediately. One day at lunch I was walking with a colleague on the other side of town when some strangers pointed to me using an unfamiliar word: "yo yung." I asked him what they were saying and he said, "Swimmer—they are calling you 'the swimmer.'" By that point, I had already forgotten about the event, but I laughed and explained my great triumph two weeks earlier.

It was around that same time that a Chinese co-worker approached me and told me that I had been invited to another swimming competition. This time, it was just me. I felt flattered and I accepted.

I arrived at a different pool with an American friend and a Chinese colleague. We didn't know anyone, and it was very hot. The longer I waited for my race to be called the more uncomfortable I felt in the heat. Finally, I was told to step up to the starting block.

When the starter's pistol rang out, I dove in and quickly realized I wasn't going to lead this time. I did my best to keep up, but I came in dead last. Worse, I was so exhausted I could barely get out of the pool. My American friend said she had never seen such fast swimmers in her life.

I didn't need the three-day incubation period to figure this one out. I had committed an offense two weeks earlier by winning three races, and for this I had to be put in my place. The second race was a setup. As punishments go, this one was relatively benign. I laughed it off because the whole exercise struck me as juvenile. I couldn't imagine anyone in the US going to such lengths to teach a foreigner a lesson *in humility. But dismissing it was my mistake: Winning a race was anything but inconsequential to my hosts.*

If this minor insult caught the attention of some local party functionary, it's safe to assume that everything from emails to web surfing does not go unnoticed today. Yet the lesson here goes beyond the internet and China. Any American doing business abroad should keep something in mind. Americans tend to walk with confidence—not arrogance, confidence—down foreign streets. It's a particular quirk in our national character and it derives, I believe, from our unusually successful history and our power. Some countries are considerably more thin-skinned and don't always view that confidence, history or power in a positive light, even when they have been its beneficiaries.

When I finally got out of the pool that afternoon, one Chinese man watching the race offered his observation: "You were very good," he said with a smile. "They were just better."

> —Warren Kozak, "Nothing in China is ever as it seems, at least for an outsider," *Wall Street Journal*, 31 March 2001

For more insights, Hou Wai-Lu's *Short History of Chinese Philosophy*, published by the Foreign Languages Press, 1959, makes a fascinating read for non-Chinese business people trading with China.

We have our own worldviews

Each culture, be it racial, national, familial, professional, or religious, creates its own set of values and beliefs. These are fed into our DNA with our mothers' milk as we grow up, and inculcated by teachers, religious leaders, parents and grandparents. All these contribute to how we see the world and how we behave. Just think for a minute about any three key messages you heard as you were growing up. As a coach one hears a wide variety, including "Being Number Two is not good enough," or "Always respect your elders and do what they tell you to do," or "Don't argue, just do it," or "Do it yourself or it will never get done."

The conjunction of multiple worldviews within a multi-cultural

Our first team meeting in Thailand with the new boss was weird. We knew the Thai colleagues did not agree with the way he wanted to merchandise our fruit and vegetables, yet they all kept quiet and did not offer any suggestions. It was only a few months later, when I and another team member from Europe learnt how important it was to respect the boss—especially as he was older than us—did I begin to understand how different it was from France.

—French CFO working in a retail operation in Bangkok

team can hence be chaotic at times. Each member interprets issues, problems, missions and visions differently, and has strict ideas about what is polite, desirable, acceptable or downright offensive. Even a seemingly simple matter such as time, which we take totally for granted in our own environments, becomes very complex when interpreted by different cultures.

In the UK, being late for a meeting—even just four or five

minutes late—is interpreted as extremely rude. Theatres close their doors at the start of a performance so that others in the audience will not be disturbed. In many other countries, such as Pakistan, Argentina and Cyprus, being half an hour late for a meeting or dinner invitation is quite acceptable. South Americans have the term *hora inglesa* ("English time") when they want someone to turn up punctually. However, they tend to be—even senior people—more generous with their time than is common in Anglo-Saxon societies, where meetings tend to finish as well as start on time, even if there's a valuable discussion developing. So, there can be a plus side to individuals not looking at their watches every few minutes.

If you understand history, you will see why time-keeping matters to the British—almost to the point of obsession. Their dominance in sea power in the 18th and 19th centuries owed much to their invention of a sea-worthy clock, the chronometer, which enabled navigators to fix longitude (Sobel 1995). They organized the world's time system, fixing Greenwich, a suburb of London, in the centre. Their Parliament is dominated by a huge clock tower, famous for its enormous bell, known as Big Ben. And traditionally, British employers give you a carriage clock as a present when you retire, though that practice is dying out.

This seemingly small issue of time-keeping is an example of the kind of thing that underlies a lot of stereotypes about how different nationalities behave. It is also a classic case of a difference that you can work around if you are adaptable, and able to see that there are advantages and disadvantages to meetings starting and finishing punctually.

There is a relatively large Indian population in Michigan. When invited to dinner in an Indian home we typically arrive half an hour to an hour late, and wouldn't dream of coming on time. With US colleagues we always ensure we are dead on time so as not to offend our hosts.

— Professor at Michigan University,
who immigrated from India in the late 1990s

Clearly, without gaining a true understanding of these issues, cross-cultural working is a minefield.

Which stories did you grow up with?

A bit of historical due diligence is always worthwhile when visiting or working in another country. There's an old saying that "One person's terrorist is another's freedom fighter." It sounds exaggerated and cynical, but it is absolutely true. For example, throughout Central and South America, the 16th-century figure Francis Drake is known as a bloodthirsty tyrant, a pirate who brought terror upon the continent and stole gold and silver. Mothers will scare their children, by saying: "If you don't eat your greens, Francis Drake will come and get you." In his home country England, however, he is revered as a war hero and a great explorer. There are statues.

In 2006 the then Japanese prime minister, Junichiro Koizumi, provoked anger in China and other Asian countries that had been occupied by the Japanese in the 1940s when he visited the Yasukuni Shrine. This shrine honours the 2.5 million war dead of Japan, but the names on the memorial include those of 14 people convicted as war criminals by a 1948 tribunal. The Chinese foreign ministry protested at the time: "This move... seriously harms the feelings of those victimized by Japanese militarism during World War II."

It is impossible to understand modern China, and the role of the Communist Party, without being aware of the history of occupation. Other countries that were occupied by the Axis powers in the 1940s, such as Korea, the Netherlands, France, Norway and so on, will have some common features in their national psyches.

For other countries, such as were occupied by the European powers in the 19th and 20th centuries, the big struggle was for independence. They are today typically bi- or multi-lingual, with an official European language for business, and local languages for everyday conversation. In a few, such as Paraguay, the native tongue—Guaraní—has near parity with Spanish and is almost universally spoken. What are the lingering effects of colonialism on these peoples' attitudes? Think, for example, how Indians might feel when they are working in a call centre for a British bank, when just a few decades ago they were dominated by that "Imperialist" country?

Many other countries have been marked by civil war. In these, typically, a revolutionary force—seeking to overturn established institutions or religions—battled against a reactionary force. Did the revolutionary side win (France, the USA, China, Russia)? Or the conservative side (Spain, Chile)? Or was the winner simultaneously revolutionary and conservative (Ireland, Iran)? Studying this is a precious guide to understanding the roles of certain institutions in the modern country. In the collective memory, incidents of a hundred years ago or more are still, in effect, recent. In the case of the USA, for example, attitudes towards racial integration and the role of the federal state still vary by region in a pattern that is similar to that of the 1860s Civil War, though rather confusingly the Republican Party has inverted its role from liberal to conservative in that time.

So, if you are showing someone around your own country, or being shown around someone else's, be aware that some of the tourist sites are historical memorials, and some of the national institutions are historical creations, and that these will have very different meanings for different people, depending on the stories they grew up with.

Spotting the soul within

It is essential to understand differences, including cultural differences; but some of these can be quite superficial. Even more important is to understand common points among people. When you get to know someone from a different culture, at the beginning it is the differences that stand out: how you greet one another; how they use cutlery; what music they listen to; how expressive they are; their sense of humour or degree of politeness. As you get to know them well, eventually you don't even notice the differences at all, and you relate purely to the personality. Of course, a cultural difference may emerge from time to time, even in a long-established friendship, but with trust and communication, it typically becomes no more than a talking point.

EXERCISES
A NEW CULTURAL LENS

So what do we need to think about when working in a different country, or when managing a multi-cultural—perhaps even international—team?

1. Think about the thoughts people may have about you and what you represent; the image of your country in their heads; your culture, your food and your religion. Write them down as if you were in their shoes. For example, what might a Zulu feel about the Afrikaners in South Africa? Or how might a Mexican feel about the Spanish conquistadores? (Most people from Mexico, Central America, Peru and Bolivia descend from native Americans, not Europeans).

2. Come to terms with the prejudices that you carry about people from other countries. Don't be shy about letting them surface and recognizing that they exist. Only then can you really connect with people who are different from you with "unconditional respect."

3. "When in Rome, do as the Romans do." Don't criticize others' religious traditions, cuisines or ways of behaving. Try to get used to their food. Attend

continued >>>

a religious service that you are unfamiliar with, to familiarize yourself with how others do things differently.

4. In many schools across the world, International Children's Day encourages children to talk in the classroom about their own backgrounds. You could do the same with your colleagues.

5. Watch foreign movies; for example, from India, Pakistan and Iran there are several classics like *Water*, *Salaam Bombay*, *Turtles Can Fly*; and from France and Spain, try *À bout de souffle*, *Jules et Jim*, *Caché*, *Todo sobre mi madre*, *Volver*, etc.

6. Watch travel programmes on TV. Most TV stations have many different kinds of these.

7. Read. There are many books and articles about cultures and countries. Some are designated in the bibliography under culture. Importantly, study those cultures where your vendors, customers and teams are located. Always read up on their history and socio-political contexts. Wikipedia is an endless source of focused, relevant information.

continued >>>

8. Learn the local customs and passions, and try to join in. For example, if you are visiting Latin America, learn at least the basic steps of salsa dancing. You will no longer feel left out at social gatherings, and you will begin to understand the music and way of life. If you are visiting India, learn the rules of cricket and the biography of Sachin Tendulkar. If you are asking yourself "Who's Sachin Tendulkar?"—then you haven't even begun to understand this country. And if you are an Indian visiting the USA, learn the rules of baseball, and go to a game.

3 TRAVEL WHENEVER YOU CAN

Travel whenever you can for fun or for work. Grab every opportunity to take an assignment in another country, even if it is for only a few weeks. Attend conferences, and visit business sites.

If you take the trouble to visit the countries related to your work, the very fact that you have made an effort will be well appreciated by your boss, customers, or potential partners. It shows a personal commitment to the project or initiative you are involved with, and will help bolster the network of relationships that you need for international working.

But even more importantly, seeing and experiencing how people live in another place is essential intelligence for working in, buying from, or selling to that particular region. Do people live with their parents and in-laws, as in India, or do single-family households predominate? Do people live in a very communal way, where they know their neighbourhood, for example in Nicaragua? Or is it much more private, where people always drive to visit friends (Los Angeles)? What is the infrastructure like? What are the distances involved? Mobile-phone operators have done well in Africa by noting a great desire to communicate and trade but a limited traditional cable communication infrastructure.

Immersion is best

The best way to gather this intelligence and experience life in another culture is total immersion. On your travels, get on a local bus or train, and mix with locals rather than staying in your "Western-style" hotel, disengaged from the local population. Immersing yourself in another culture is the best way to understand it.

Enlightened companies understand the importance of "going native" in another location. Samsung, for example, in 1991 established its Global Management Development Institute, offering courses in international business management, history, culture and economics, as well as language training. The idea is that the learning occurs at many levels—not only in the classroom but through conversations with participants from different regions. In the programme, selected trainees choose a country, undergo three months of intensive language and cross-cultural training, and then spend a year in that country. They have no specific job assignment and—an interesting detail—are forbidden to make contact with the local Samsung office. They are also encouraged to travel by road, on buses or trains, because in that way they see more of the country and have more opportunity to interact with local people (Gupta & Govindarajan, "Cultivating a Global Mind-set").

At first, the experience of immersion can be isolating and bruising. There will be frustrating, even humiliating, experiences in shops, banks and restaurants where you cannot get what you ordered and people make little effort to help you. These teething pains exist with all learning; you will have experienced the same in your studies in medicine, law, engineering or whatever your initial qualification was. It's worth working through this pain barrier and coming through the other side.

Act global, think local

Although travel is the best way to truly get under the skin of another culture, not everyone can travel frequently, or attend international conferences, or do a three-month placement in another country, let alone be posted abroad for several years at a stretch. Most people have at least some ties to their family and community that limit their mobility. Many partners may have good career opportunities at the home base, so relocating might not be possible. In addition to child-care and education, increasing numbers of people have to look after elderly parents, as longevity increases in many countries. Recent economic problems have also dented many travel budgets.

In the Web 2.0 world, however, there are numerous ways to maintain an international network of friends and business contacts even while your ability to travel is limited. For example, some business networking sites, such as Ecademy, have a widely dispersed membership, with participants looking to connect on the basis of shared interests, rather than geographical location.

Even learning another language can be done locally. Not only is the internet a source of learning, but if you are perfecting one of the more widely spoken languages, it can be worth checking online if there is a native speaker of Mandarin, Portuguese or Russian living close to you. If there are limits to your ability to travel, learning a language actually becomes even more important, as it's a way of getting to know people, both locally and through the internet, extending your network as well as your knowledge. You can make genuine friendships and useful business relationships in this way, even if you never actually meet in person.

One valuable source of interaction is an initiative called the World Café Community (www.theworldcafe.com). It is a global initiative, which now runs online, and has members from North and South America, Western and Central Europe, and Asia, who debate and discuss many work and management issues. It began in English, but there are now sub-groups where members chat in other languages. At the time of writing it also offers Spanish, German, Indonesian, Portuguese, Russian, and Italian-speaking groups. The ethos is based on sharing ideas for community, teamwork and tackling social and environmental problems. It's not exclusively related to workplace matters, but it is a valuable source of conversations on these and many other issues. It "feels" a little more like a community than some social media platforms—though

I would like to do more traveling, but in this current economic climate, travel is the first thing that has been affected, and most people in this area are doing less and less. I, like many others, am now primarily using the internet to network for business. The only trouble is that this generates the urge for more travel! The internet is most definitely a vital tool in discovering more about an area you have not visited, but sooner or later you will have to "get your feet on the ground" so to speak... hence the need to travel again.

—British businesswoman,
working in the holiday industry in Thailand

personal preference on all such sites is the final determinant. Discussions may stay online, or become supported by face-to-face meetings. For example, the Café Latino has planned a series of meetings in Colombia, Argentina and Brazil for 2010, with the agenda for discussion posted on a Google Document.

As video-conferencing and "avatar-style" virtual-interaction technology improve, there will be more ways to engage with others in another country without having to fly.

Relocating for work

The Welsh footballer Ian Rush, who spent a year playing in the Italian Serie A league, was once famously quoted as saying: "I couldn't settle in Italy—it was like living in a foreign country."

Relocating can be tough, and takes guts. Some enjoy it more than others. Those who nervously seek out fellow expatriates, and try to buy the food that they eat at home, will find it harder than others who enthusiastically embrace new cultural experiences.

Planning your exit, mapping your entry

Take out the stress, when beginning your move, by careful planning and attention to detail. Leave no stone unturned, and you will end up with no unpleasant surprises. Below is a list of some of the "Must Dos" and "Must Haves" that you would be advised to take care of:

Contract: Before you leave, make sure that your new work contract has clarity on every front. Be careful of clauses like "You will receive a car commensurate with your job level" or "Your apartment rental will be in line with your job band." Be specific about the model and type of car, and make sure your housing allowance will suit you and your family. Make sure the neighbourhood or location you will be in suits schooling and travel needs. It is very easy to land up in a dump. In places where traffic travels very slowly, make sure you know how long it actually takes to get to school or work, rather than merely how far it is. A kilometre in Mumbai sometimes take as long as fifteen minutes to half an hour.

Passport: Make sure all passports are valid for more than six months. If you plan to be away for longer than six months, it is worth applying for a new one. Visas, too, are usually required when working in another country, except for citizens of the European Union working in another EU country.

Driving license: Check that your driving license is valid in the country you are relocating to. You might be required to take a driving test. If you are moving from one state to another in the USA, you might be required to take the knowledge test... again.

Medical reports: Take your medical and dental reports and X-rays if you have them, and make sure you have the inoculations that are appropriate and necessary for the region.

Banking: Advise your bank as to your plans so that you can do all your banking online. This is especially important if you will be transferring money back to the home base or required to make any direct debits or automatic payments.

Properties: If you are putting your home on the market, either to rent or sell, make sure you have a good realtor or estate agent to provide appropriate support. It is also a great time to get rid of any clothes, gadgets, or household goods that you don't use any more. Many charity shops and house clearance companies don't take electrical appliances and mattresses, so you might have to dump some of these. Remember that around the world there are different voltages and electric sockets and plugs, so some appliances might not work in the country you are moving to. You can find buyers online, on networks such as eBay and Craigslist.

Saying goodbye: Make sure you say your goodbyes to colleagues, customers, vendors. While away, work hard to keep these networks going. They will stay important and often very useful to you.

The home front: Family and friends will need a lot of support from you. Many will feel sad that you are leaving, and family members moving with you might be feeling quite vulnerable too. But don't forget "you." Find someone to share all that you are going through, but make sure you stay away from people who keep telling you what a bad move you are making, thus aggravating your own anxieties.

When you get there

There are a number of "Must Dos" which are top priority to get out of the way, and which can often be cumbersome and bureaucratic:

The law: Please remember that laws and regulations do differ from country to country. Importantly, never get on the wrong side of the law—you could face a felony charge or even deportation. For example, in the USA, when driving, not only the driver, but passengers too, are not allowed to drink alcohol; in fact, closed as well as open cans or bottles of alcohol may not be kept in the car at all in most states. There are many countries where this is perfectly acceptable.

Registration: In some countries, you have to register your arrival with the immigration or police authorities. In India, for example, this is a legal requirement.

Banking: Preferably bank with an international bank to ensure that money transfers either way are easily facilitated. Sort out credit cards and cash cards. In the USA, building up a credit history to attain a credit card takes up to a year.

Driving test: If you are driving, many countries require you to take a driving test within a minimum time period. In the USA, for example, some states require formal registration and often testing as well.

GPS: Get yourself a navigation system for the car; it takes the stress out of map-reading and getting lost.

Phone and internet: Sort out your communication media quickly, so you can call and email friends and family with ease. There are many really cheap carriers for international calling, and Skype is wonderful for free internet calls. Understanding different mobile-phone options is often extremely complex, so check them out carefully so that you don't run high phone bills. If you are staying in a hotel beware of exorbitant calling charges from your room.

Medical treatment: Find out where the best hospitals and doctors are—while you are healthy. There is nothing worse than trying to find a good doctor when you really need one, whether for emergency treatment or medication. In some remote locations it is a good idea to keep a couple of disposable syringes with you just in case they are not available. Always make sure these are opened in full view, to ensure sterilized instrumentation.

Live like a local: Avoid being closeted in an expat community. There is at times a tendency to moan about the locals, the place, the food. Locals are much more likely to be knowledgeable about the best places to eat and shop. Remember, "you don't know what you don't know," and you could be in for some wonderful surprises.

And at work

Induction: Plan a really good induction for yourself. Many companies run induction programmes, but even these sometimes miss out on some of the important things you need to know. Take the time to connect with and understand the new work culture. Sometimes it is as simple as what time people typically come to work, what they do for lunch, and when they leave.

Networking: In your first 90 days in the job, focus on building networks and relationships with people you will be working with—colleagues, bosses, team members, vendors, customers, and external networks such as government officials. Importantly, ask loads of questions, and listen to what they have to say. Don't be tempted to jump the gun and make big changes, criticize and complain too often, or too soon. If you rock the boat too quickly, you might just be the first one overboard.

Workplace culture: Study the culture of the workplace as well as the country or location. The same organization can have quite a different culture in different parts of the world. Even companies such as Johnson & Johnson, Unilever, Coca-Cola and Pepsi, which insist on the same quality assurance worldwide, display a variety of work cultures, influenced by local habits and behaviours.

Prioritize: Create clarity around you as to what your priorities are, as well as your short- and longer-term plans. Share these with the people you will be working with.

Family: Take special care not to neglect the family. Children will be struggling with their own transition with schooling and friends. Your spouse or partner might land up dealing with a lot of the "stuff" that needs to be done, often feeling vulnerable and anxious.

Staying positive: Don't worry if at the beginning there are times when you are filled with self-doubt, confusion, and anxiety. These are perfectly normal feelings, all connected to the overall transition.

When I started working in Shanghai, I realized to my dismay that this was not going to be as easy as I thought, despite the fact that, as far as organized retail operations go, I am really pretty good. If only I had taken the time to understand more about how Confucian ideals and the overall Chinese culture are intertwined in the way Chinese do business, life would have been much easier and business performance much stronger.

The US is a far more individualistic culture, and my style in retrospect was far too aggressive for people who honour harmony. Our business would have gotten off to a much better start if I had paid more attention to building relationships rather than just building stores and sales figures.

—Executive in a US corporate,
working in China as Head of Operations

Accept the times when you are thinking, "Is this really a good idea?" or "If only I had stayed where I was." Just let these anxious feelings flow in and out; after a while they will get less and less as you settle in.

Staying in touch: Don't forget to stay in touch with the old gang. Your networks will have expanded and it is important not to neglect your ex-colleagues. Email makes staying connected so easy, and social networks such as Twitter, LinkedIn or Facebook, even easier.

Plan your return

Many international postings are of limited duration, and it's common to return to your country of origin. This can be as difficult, albeit in different ways, as your initial relocation.

Career progression: To begin with, you need to plan how your return fits in with your career. Ideally, there is an opportunity at least as valuable as the one that caused you to relocate in the first place. If you give up a promising posting because you feel homesick, it's likely that you will quickly come to regret the move. The pleasure of seeing sights and experiences that you missed from home is likely to pass quickly, while the impact of diminished career prospects will be long-lasting.

Culture shock: What you won't have expected is that there will be little culture shocks as you return—especially if you have immersed yourself in the new culture. Some of the customs you grew up with, and accepted as "normal," may suddenly appear quite eccentric. You may miss many aspects of your newer way of life. Also, while you've been away, life won't have stood still. There will be new buildings, new local celebrities, new items of gossip and news—even new turns of phrase in the local vernacular that will be unfamiliar. Some of the controversies that occupy the minds of the locals will seem trivial to you, especially if you are returning from a region experiencing more momentous events. Many of the news items won't have reached you, so you will have missed out on part of the country's collective memory. The newspapers, shops, restaurants and accents will be at once familiar and strange. It can be a surprisingly unsettling experience, and you will feel somewhat "on the outside" for a while after returning. This is a more surprising experience—after all, it is "your" culture! And you won't have expected to have to prepare for it. But it's worth doing some preparation. As indicated above, it's a good idea to stay in close touch with friends and family "back home." Shortly before or after returning, prepare one or two long conversations about everything you've missed.

Maintaining links: By the same token, do maintain contact with colleagues and friends from the posting, after you have returned. The good news is that there are now so many more means of communication for doing this than there were even two years ago. Keeping up this contact is particularly important if you have learned a language and wish to maintain proficiency. You will be surprised at how quickly your capacity declines without regular practice.

4 LEARN A LANGUAGE

"Learning the language" was the personal development most cited by respondents to the survey which would support the journey to becoming a global worker. It was second only to the importance of living and working in a country beyond the mother country. The two are closely linked. In combination, they will allow you to truly experience life and witness business from a different point of the globe. Understanding different worldviews, winning respect and gaining empathy and sympathy all stem from making an effort at conversation in another language. Your international network is instantly broadened and strengthened. One respondent noted:

> *It would be a valuable initiative just to have at least some knowledge.*
> *To learn multiple languages [would help me be a global manager].*
> *Even a little understanding of that will create a great impact.*

Then when asked "Which of the factors other than national or religious background are the biggest challenge for multi-national teamwork, according to you?" the top four factors cited were:

1. Language barriers (30 per cent)
2. Working across time zones (28 per cent)
3. Pronunciation and accent issues (21 per cent)
4. Cultural differences (16 per cent)

It was striking that language topped the list, and a language-related matter came third.

In a further dipstick study carried out among 36 managers, mainly expatriates, working in Thailand and Egypt, accent was similarly quoted as being a real hindrance to communication. The challenge of improving language and listening skills dominated the replies. Typical aspirations were:

- *Improving my language skills in languages other than English.*

- *Being able to speak more foreign languages.*

- *Learning local language and adopting local culture.*

- *Learning the language and communication style which suits that country.*

- *Knowledge and training about the political and economic climate, as well as language and culture of the market in question.*

- *Learning foreign languages other than English; courses in international business administration.*

- *Accents are a real struggle for me, especially when we all speak English, and think we understand one another, when in reality we don't.*

Before setting out on the challenge, it helps to ask: What is the purpose of learning this language? If it is to gain sufficient fluency to converse deeply and conduct business negotiations in the new tongue, then only years of learning, including immersion in the other culture, can prepare you. But even if it is to just learn enough to make greetings in the other language, break the ice (a very English metaphor) at business receptions or wedding festivities, understand a little of the local culture, and follow road signs and newspaper headlines—that is still valuable knowledge.

English is not enough

In the business world, the most common tongue is English as a second language (ESL). Every day, thousands of business meetings are conducted in English without a single native speaker being present.

But while command of English is necessary in most regions— and English-language teaching is intensifying in schools around the world—English alone is not sufficient for you to be able to operate in the global economy. In China and Brazil, for example, English is rarely spoken, compared to a country like India, where it is mostly the business language of the day. In the Mediterranean, knowledge of Arabic, French or Italian can be more useful than English in some trade shows and meetings. In parts of Africa, the common languages are French or Portuguese, in addition to the local languages. So one has to be careful not to assume that most workers are already competent in the lingua franca of the commercial world.

Learning the local language is thus first and foremost an invaluable tool for communicating with non-English-speaking contacts. But it is also much more than that. For the Global You, learning other languages has a host of extra, *hidden* advantages:

1. Enhanced cognitive ability—*it makes you sharper*
2. Enhanced interpersonal skills—*it is all about connecting*
3. Enhanced understanding—*a deeper listening*
4. Enhanced PR—*they like you more*
5. Enhanced cultural intelligence—*it all makes more sense*
6. Enhanced global network—*you meet more people*

Enhanced cognitive ability

Curiously, until the 1960s, in the English-speaking academic world, it was widely thought that being raised bilingual was detrimental to the development of cognitive ability. Then in 1962 a ground-breaking study overturned these assumptions. The psychologists Peal and Lambert found that "bilinguals scored more highly than monolinguals in both verbal and non-verbal measurements of intelligence." They argued that bilinguals "had a more diversified structure of intelligence and greater mental flexibility, and that therefore the cognitive functioning of bilinguals benefited from their bi-cultural experience, and from positive transfer between languages" (C. Hoffman, *An Introduction to Bilingualism*).

Children who are raised bilingual tend to have stronger all-round mental capacity and ability for language. Far from diluting their ability in the dominant tongue, the discipline enhances the capability of the brain to cope with advanced vocabulary and sentence construction. It also teaches an awareness of the different ways in which ideas can be verbally conveyed—for example, the diverse grammatical structures and nuances of expression.

Most studies have looked at learning a second language as a child. The reality for most global workers, however, is learning a second, third or fourth language as an adult. As is well known, the capacity for adopting new languages does diminish with age. The ability to absorb new information, particularly in language, peaks at around age five. But though it tapers off, it doesn't fall to zero. Neural pathways are more "hard-wired" by adulthood than in childhood, but they are not completely inflexible. The adult brain just has to work harder. Some of the latest research in neuro-science is uncovering the astonishingly complex and elastic properties of the human brain.

The discipline of learning a new language—and the systematic exercises required of you—results in increased working memory and improved cognitive performance. Continual, daily dedication to cognitive development helps you throughout your life to maintain and enhance mental capacity.

Enhanced interpersonal skills

Learning a few phrases of the local language helps to break the ice at initial gatherings. It shows that you care, and it creates a talking point. It helps to get the interpersonal connection going. And locals really like and respect the fact that you have made an effort to learn the language.

But there is another, less direct, benefit to learning a foreign language: it develops and heightens your general powers of listening and communicating.

Consider some of the key attributes required when learning another tongue: How well do we listen? Are we attuned to the emotion, as well as verbal content, of the individual we are conversing with? Are we aware of nuances of meaning? Can we sensitively check that we have a shared understanding of certain phrases or concepts? Do we "bond" and make the maximum effort to communicate with one another? Have we made sure that we listened through the accents, and really understood what was being said, rather than what we *thought* was being said?

It was clear watching a group of Italians from a large European engineering firm negotiating a road-building project in north India, that neither side really understood the other even though they were both speaking English. The Europeans, as they got more and more frustrated, gesticulated and raised their voices. The Indian locals couldn't understand what all the fuss was about. Neither side thought it was important to recognize the impact they were having on the others. No wonder the project landed up being deferred for six months until a facilitator assisted them to understand one another!

Learning a language helps fine-tune your emotional intelligence. When you vocabulary is limited, non-verbal communication becomes a matter of acute importance. We all know that the verbal content of a message is only a part of how you communicate, and matters such as energy, body language and intonation are of huge significance. This is the case even where the people communicating with one another are fluent in the language of discourse. It becomes even more so in the early stages of learning a language. If you concentrate solely on trying to decipher and mentally translate every word, you tend to fall behind and get lost. If you can "read" the emotion, and gather at least some of the vocabulary, you are more likely to comprehend the core of the message. A gesture, a raising of eyebrows, a gesticulation, can send very strong messages across the table. As a language-learner, you will be especially alert to these nuances; much less will "get lost in translation."

Of course, it helps to check back that you have understood correctly; but such conscientiousness and sensitivity will come naturally to someone high in emotional intelligence.

Enhanced understanding

The capacity for language-learning to enhance understanding between different peoples can be illustrated by the subtleties of translating from one language to another. The different European languages, for example, are characterized by numerous "false friends"—words that sound or look the same, but mean different things. *Actuellement* in French doesn't mean "actually," it means "at the present point in time." *Molestar* in Spanish doesn't mean to molest or rape, but simply to bother or annoy. Sometimes, the differences are subtle ones of degree: "Mist" in English means a mild haze in the sky, but in Dutch it means "fog"—so the *mist* in the Netherlands can be enough to delay your flight. In the 1980s, the BBC television news once led on a story of a Portuguese minister complaining that he had been "deceived" by the British prime minister, Margaret Thatcher. The individual looked rather baffled at being invited to the studio to explain his comments, especially at being made the lead item, and played the incident down. The newsreader quickly moved on to the next item. It was probably the case that the minister had merely meant to say he had felt "disappointment" (*deçepçao*), and either made an error with his English, or was translated incorrectly.

Some words can be translated with technical accuracy, but still mean something different owing to culture. In the US, which has a history of enterprise leading to economic growth, the terms "businessman," "entrepreneur," and so on, are positive. In Greece, which has a left-wing voter bias following right-wing dictatorships, the equivalent term is *kerdoscopos*, or "profit-maker," which is pejorative.

Even simple idiomatic expressions, if literally interpreted, can be sources of confusion. A banker from Tanzania, working for a British bank, who relocated to London, recalls:

> *When I first started working in London, I was very confused as to why every evening when people left the office they said "See you later," yet they did not attempt to make plans to meet in the evening. It was only months later that someone explained it was just a way of saying "goodbye," or a sort of "au revoir."*

Those who have learned another language, and worked extensively in a region not of their birth and upbringing, are more likely to take the time to double-check that there is a mutually shared understanding of key phrases and terms. They will take special care if the words are of crucial importance—in a contract, for example.

How many business relationships have been affected by such translation ambiguities and errors? All the examples above underline how important it is to check there is a common understanding. The person in an international meeting who's bold enough to say: "Sorry, I'm not sure I quite understand that term" risks sounding ignorant, but is often providing a valuable service to all team members. Don't be shy to confirm you understood correctly. Use the phrase "My understanding is…. Is that correct?" This simple discipline saves hours of painful discussion—or, worse, a course of action based on a profound misunderstanding.

Enhanced PR

Making an effort to learn the language of the individual or group you are doing business with generates enormous goodwill.

Executive Jeroen Elbertse, who is from the Netherlands, and has learned English, German and "a little" French and Spanish, comments: "It helps to put an effort into learning the local language. You need not necessarily master the language, but it will help, and in general be appreciated by your business partners."

Robert Barzelay, a Dutch/Israeli national who has relocated 35 times, lived in 12 different countries, and visited, mostly for work, close to 100 countries, is managing partner of Global Strategists. He speaks English and Dutch as mother tongues, and French fluently. He has also learned a good or moderate level of German, Spanish and Hebrew. Based on the experience of all this international working, his advice is: "Even if you don't speak a language, I always try to learn the 20 to 30 basic words or sentences in the language of the country I visit. It's good PR. Even if you totally goof in the pronunciation, it's always good for a laugh. People are very sensitive

EXECUTING CUSTOMERS IN STRICT ROTATION
and other translating gems

Some of these have been published before, but we just couldn't resist...

- **In a Bangkok dry cleaner's:** Drop your trousers here for best results.

- **In an East African newspaper:** A new swimming pool is rapidly taking shape since the contractors have thrown in the bulk of their workers.

- **In a Zurich hotel:** Because of the impropriety of entertaining guests of the opposite sex in the bedroom, it is suggested that the lobby be used for this purpose.

- **In an advertisement by a Hong Kong dentist:** Teeth extracted by the latest Methodists.

- **In a Rome laundry:** Ladies, leave your clothes here and spend the afternoon having a good time.

- **In the window of a Swedish furrier:** Fur coats made for ladies from their own skin.

continued >>>

- **In a Czechoslovakian tourist agency:** Take one of our horse-driven city tours—we guarantee no miscarriages.

- **In a Copenhagen airline ticket office:** We take your bags and send them in all directions.

- **In a Norwegian cocktail lounge:** Ladies are requested not to have children in the bar.

- **At a Budapest zoo:** Please do not feed the animals. If you have any suitable food, give it to the guard on duty.

- **In an Acapulco hotel:** The manager has personally passed all the water served here.

- **From a brochure of a car rental firm in Tokyo:** When passenger of foot heave in sight, tootle the horn. Trumpet him melodiously at first, but if he still obstacles your passage then tootle him with vigor.

- **In a Rhodes tailor shop:** Order your summers suit. Because is big rush we will execute customers in strict rotation.

for their language, and that little effort you show can open doors or melt the ice in tough encounters."

Consider also this observation from the local manager of a chemical manufacturing plant in Indonesia:

The expats had basically been running the company over here in Indonesia for over ten years. Although some of us spoke English, a lot of the staff were much more comfortable expressing their ideas and thoughts in our mother tongue, Bahasa Indonesia. I wouldn't have expected them to learn some of the local dialects or Javanese, but honestly, they didn't even try to learn some of the basics, like "How are you?" or "Could we please discuss these items?" It really alienated us from them.

Corporate office tried to put in some succession planning for us locals to grow into senior roles. But the expat bosses kept saying we weren't ready or good enough. How could they know if they didn't bother to connect with almost all the workforce?

It's always worth having at least some knowledge of the language of a region you're visiting or doing business with, to build a good rapport with the people there.

And this does not entail having to be a "master" of the language —if such a thing is even possible. No native Russian or Japanese speaker could master Castilian Spanish to the level of Gabriel García Márquez. But then the same is true of any Spanish-speaking person. A similar reservation among language-learners is to think "Why bother learning the basic phrases in Mandarin? I don't have time to learn it properly and I'll never be fluent." But language ability is not binary. It doesn't consist of the two categories, "ignorance" and "fluency." There are *degrees* of fluency, including for native speakers.

If you have spent months or years learning a language, only to experience a frustrating hour and a half in a cinema understanding little of a movie, you could think "Why did I bother?" But you could also think for a moment of the advantages it affords you. You can ask for items in a shop, hold conversations with people who make an effort to understand you, and read the local newspaper. And at the very least, you can—with just simple phrases, greetings and compliments—generate the goodwill among your interlocutors that will greatly smoothen the process of working in a foreign land.

Enhanced cultural intelligence

Languages are constructed in very different ways; there aren't always directly equivalent terms. For this reason, we are fond of taking out words we like from other languages on long-term loan. Many languages adopt English business terms such as "networking" and "software," while English is just as predatory, pinching "Kindergarten" and "Zeitgeist" from German, "ego" and "charisma" and "democracy" from Greek; "rapprochement," "detente" and many others from French. To begin with, in written form, they are often italicized to denote their status as tenants rather than freeholders in the host language, but after an unofficial qualifying period, we eventually adopt them as our own. Some words like "OK" and "taxi" are now pretty much universal.

Grammar, as well as vocabulary, is diverse, and often reflects national attitudes. The subjunctive mood, as used in verbs, denotes ambiguity, contingency, possibility. It is uncommon in English, and of declining popularity in French, but all the rage in Spanish, where it doubles up as the most popular form of the imperative. This polite form of expressing an order as just a suggestion is engaging. It seems to reflect a more laid-back culture in Hispanic countries than you find in Germanic and Anglo-Saxon ones. You will see a connection with a more direct use of language in northern countries with a stronger emphasis on punctuality. So here the grammar really is a clue to the culture.

Languages also vary in the way they refer to geographic entities. Here, the influence of politics and history is evident. Understanding such subtle variations is a valuable part of becoming a global thinker and global worker. It can be dangerous territory. The word "America" in spoken English refers to the fifty states of the USA, rather than its technical definition, that is, the continent that stretches from the Bering Strait to Tierra del Fuego. A definition that treats the USA and America as synonyms has passed into common usage across the world. In Spanish, the term *América*, with the accent on the *e*, means the whole continent; so Buenos Aires is no less American than Texas or New York. The Spanish have, however, the adjective *estadounidense*, which has no direct equivalent in English. Literally, it translates as "United States-ish," and is used to refer to that which is characteristic of the Union of fifty states.

The 20th century was the "American" century, dominated by the USA's financial and military power, and the use of the term "America" as synonymous with its most powerful country reflected this. If the relative importance of the USA diminishes in the 21st century, it will be interesting to see if this interchangeability of the terms "USA" and "America" in the English language and others begins to be weakened. Vocabulary, as it turns out, can be a good barometer of world politics.

These considerations link closely with the exercise in Chapter 1—tipping up the globe and looking at it from a new angle. From which perspective do you look at the world? Does Europe or Asia loom largest in your consciousness? When you hear the word "America," do you think solely of the fifty states of "America," or the broad, diverse continent "América" that runs almost from North to South Pole?

When undertaking an exercise such as this, there is yet a danger that a re-orientated perspective becomes solidified into a new orthodoxy. It can be stifling for international communication if there is a perceived "right" and "wrong" terminology, backed up by politically correct rule-making and enforcement, denouncing, for example, the instinct among native English speakers to refer to America as a country, especially as there is an absence of an alternative in the adjectival form. There is a tendency in human behaviour to see competition for ideas as a fight to the death, where a healthier instinct is to tolerate debate, dissent and alternative perspectives.

The purpose of this chapter is to illuminate that language and communication difficulties highlight different global perspectives. The struggle is to view the world through different lenses and engage with others as if you were really in their shoes. Culturally alternative "maps" of the world's human geography are often

THE ARROGANCE OF THE NATIVE ENGLISH SPEAKER

Those of us who grew up speaking English seem to carry natural advantages with us to the world of global work. We do not suffer the difficulties that others do in following a talk, or a contribution at a meeting, from someone with rapid speech or a difficult accent. We can often find someone who understands us, at least on a basic level. We can access sources of news and comment in English from just about anywhere in the world.

There are two unfortunate results to this "advantage," however. The first is that the entire exercise in figuratively tipping the world upside-down and looking at it from a different cultural standpoint is, for us, an optional—not compulsory—part of the business education curriculum. We hence have to make greater effort to access all the multiple dimensions of enhanced awareness and intellectual growth that come from immersion in another language.

Secondly, it unfortunately gives rise to arrogance among some native English speakers, who expect everyone to communicate in English. Such colonial attitudes don't go down well. Native English speakers need to make more effort to communicate with others and understand matters from their perspective. (Those who do make that effort, however, sometimes find themselves in an ironic situation when they begin to address someone in their native tongue: on hearing the accent, the individual often replies in English!)

strongly internalized into the collective unconscious of different regions and languages. There are multiple such views. The experience of the authors and the people we have interviewed does not constitute a unified, universal view, so our examples are illustrative, not exhaustive. Learning languages, especially when accompanied by complete immersion in another country and culture, can be an enriching experience, but it affords a different, rather than necessarily superior, point of view. The fresh perspective is complementary, not in competition.

Learning a foreign language can spur you to perfect your own language, as you learn the endless possibilities for discovery. The German philosopher Johann Wolfgang von Goethe observed: "The person who knows only one language does not truly know that language." The experience of deep immersion in another language helps you understand that there is no ceiling to improving your mastery, and this is true of your own language also. A fuller knowledge of how language works improves your capability in all those that you speak. Even more importantly, for the purposes of global working, it equips you to be sensitive to others in communication, to listen well. If someone makes a mistake, you're more likely to endeavour to find out what they were *trying* to say— and what it might mean in their culture, rather than yours.

Enhanced global network

The final advantage of learning other languages is fairly obvious: an enhanced global network—for there will be more online social networking groups that you can participate in. Normally, face-to-face meetings are better for communication, but in a language in which you are not yet fluent, online networks have the advantage of allowing you to check the words as you type, and check the dictionary as you read. No one is timing you.

You can connect with many different groups. As noted in the previous chapter, the World Café now has sub-groups in Spanish, French, Portuguese, Indonesian, German, Dutch (though some of the conversations in the Benelux group are in English) and Russian. LinkedIn is available in a growing number of languages. At the time of writing, this is just four—English, French, Spanish and German—but the organizers are planning expansion. Nico Posner, writing on the LinkedIn blog in June 2009, noted that more than half of the 42 million people on the network are from outside the network's home base of the USA. He added: "A frequent request from our members is to offer the LinkedIn website in their native language." This request is consistent with the results of the surveys on which this book is based, which is that while English is the main language for business in many countries, increasing multi-lingual channels, and increasing language ability by individuals, are valuable developments for global working.

So Nico asked the linguists on LinkedIn for their preferred incentive for helping him with translations. An upgraded LinkedIn account was the most popular, cited by 45 per cent of respondents. But the other preferences cited shed useful light on the ambitions of global workers:

1.   Ability to highlight your translation work on your
     LinkedIn profile (38 per cent)
2.   Membership of the LinkedIn Translation Group
     (30 per cent)
3.   Translation leader board recognition (21 per cent)
4.   I would want to do this because it's fun (18 per cent)

The last of these is intriguing. Much of the effort that goes into global networking, by busy international workers with pressures and deadlines, is motivated by pure interest: the intellectual challenge of translating and developing expertise and knowledge, combined with the fun of connecting with other people.

There is a lot of research on networking, neuro-science, emotional intelligence and doubtless other disciplines that supports the idea that learning new languages greatly enhances our ability to operate as global players. The same applies to deepening our understanding of the ones we do speak. Such learning comes more naturally to those who recognize the importance of connecting with people who are different from them—in language and in worldview—and who demonstrate the discipline of continual learning, of treating every day as a lesson. We'll discuss this subject more in the next chapter.

STRATEGIES FOR LEARNING A LANGUAGE

Before moving to the region of the language you're learning:

- Seize every opportunity to improve your language skills.
- Take proper lessons; they should ideally be more than once a week. Learn grammar and begin conversations as soon as you can.
- Learn the vocabulary of the subject you will mostly be dealing in—shipping, finance, textiles, etc.
- Be clear about the reason for learning another language—but remember that you don't have to be fluent for it to be useful.

Once you are working in the new location:

- Don't just rely on learning casually through everyday conversations; continue lessons, study and practise.
- Listen to the local radio and watch local TV stations. News will be the first you are able to understand— drama and, especially, comedy are more challenging.
- As soon as you can, start to converse and think in the new language, including with travel or work companions. You may be two Russians living in Paris, but speak French to each other all the time—even when you're just chatting about what to get for dinner. It will feel strange to begin with, but this is the route to real mastery.

continued >>>

- Focus on your accent, speak slowly and clearly when talking to others, and ask them to do the same... please.
- Absorb as much as you can of the different worldview that the new language represents.
- Persevere. You may feel frustrated for weeks or months, but there will come a day when you pass a tipping point, and you will comprehend most of what is said. The first joke that you "get," the first dream in the language—these are advanced landmarks. It's worth all the effort for these breakthrough moments.
- Remember: lingual ability is not binary. It isn't on or off. It's a continual, learning experience.

And after you have returned:

- Continually improve your capability in the languages you already speak—including your native tongue!
- Use your language skills to build online networks, spend dedicated time continuing to practise and learn.

5 LEARN TO LEARN OUT OF THE CLASSROOM

To do anything well, claims Malcolm Gladwell in *The Outliers*, it takes at least 10,000 hours. The figure may be disputed, but to anyone who has learned to play a musical instrument, or to reach advanced level in golf or the tango or—as we discussed in the previous chapter—another language, it feels about right. If you want to get to Carnegie Hall, as the old saying goes, "honey you gotta practise!"

For the Global You, practice is one of the keys to developing relevant leadership skills. Whether for functional or behavioural skills, as managers we may get the occasional course or series of coaching interventions; other than that, we are on our own. But do we take the time to practise? Most of us jump back into the day-to-day list of "To Do's," and neglect to spend the time making sure that the new learning "sticks."

In response to this, more organizations are recognizing the need to introduce action learning approaches, to ensure that there is real engagement in learning not only from HR, but from participants and bosses as well. If you are the boss, it is in fact you who should be encouraging people to learn, and finding projects where they can apply and practise what they have learnt, whether it be a specific project to practise new project management skills, or a financial planning initiative to practise new financial modelling techniques.

Without practice, none of the learning methods we're introducing in this chapter will be of any good.

Cut out inefficient learning

Most of us have spent hours or even days listening to boring lectures or presentations about various topics related to work, management skills and leadership. Most of the time, it hasn't been much fun. When we returned to the "day job," hundreds of emails, and work that had piled up, took days to clear. Often the boss wasn't really interested in what we had learnt, or able to understand how important it was to begin using it on the job.

There is a tendency to assume that "all learning is good," but there can actually be much misdirected time and effort:

> *I received an email from HR telling me that I had been nominated to attend a workshop on financial modeling. Being an "IT man," I had no clue why, or to what purpose. During the classroom training, I found myself surrounded by people from the strategy and finance teams, and couldn't quite work out what I was doing there. I had no interest in the topic and found the four-day event very boring. That was just over two years ago, and I haven't applied any of it to my job.*
>
> — Chan W., working for a large global bank

So, maybe you, too, were not quite sure why you had been sent on a particular training course, and didn't manage to put it to good use anyway. Most people tell us that after a workshop, the 360-degree feedback, or negative feedback on interpersonal skills, was often put in the "bottom drawer," never to be looked at again, except if requested by HR, or in times of "crisis." The latter might include job termination or being passed over for a promotion. In a recent series of advanced workshops that a world-class faculty ran for a group of managers, most of the participants could not recollect their "scores" on 360-degree competency feedback, as well as their leadership and learning styles on most dimensions—which they had studied for the foundation-level program just 12 months earlier. Most admitted that they had not followed through on the action planning and that not much had changed. This was despite the fact that all had rated the program very highly, and left committed to work on their particular behavioural areas identified.

As Peter Senge, an authority on learning in organizations and with individuals, observes: "If nothing concrete happens within 30 days after a session, nothing will ever happen."

Research tells us that the actual transfer of learning from training to the workplace is very low, and that, over time, little is remembered by the audience, the prime reason being lack of practice. Some research even suggests that transfer failure is as high as 90 per cent for some training courses (Garavaglia 1955; Georgenson 1982; Broad & Newstrom 1992). Of course, much of this is denied by trainers, who on the other hand mostly struggle to identify what percentage of training actually transfers to the job.

Learn to learn out of the classroom

What we do know today is that learning for adults must be relevant, engaging, participative, fun, and tailored to individual learning styles. Preferences include learning by observation, reading, reflecting and actually doing. Most managers and Chief Learning Officers will tell you that working on projects and simulations in small groups is often

BECOME A GLOBAL LEARNER:
A CASE-STUDY

When Pedro Havez was nominated to attend a Strategic Leadership Program at a top leadership institute he assumed it would be "just another" of those training programs: Read up a case study, participate a bit in the classroom, network with some interesting colleagues and learn about those aspects of strategy that he had struggled to understand in a book. He was in for a pleasant surprise.

1. First, he had to complete an e-learning program. No completion, no attendance.
2. Then, one whole day was spent on preparing participants to work in multi-functional, multi-national and multi-cultural groups.
3. Classroom teaching was highly participative, with intensive engagement and breakout work in groups.
4. Participants were taught specific models that would ensure a common language, common frameworks and common approach.
5. Simulations and outbound exercises were used to enhance assimilation of the learnings.
6. Participants were then broken up into teams of 5-6, with members encouraged to learn about one another's strengths, and agree on individual and team accountabilities.

continued >>>

7. They were taught how to function in virtual, matrix teams, to learn about team norms and values, culture-building and communication.

8. At the end of the week, they departed, clear about the deliverables demanded by the faculty, and ready to start working on real live projects.

9. Over the next 16 weeks, the journey was not easy. The teams had to work virtually, with people from other countries, on top of their day jobs.

10. Although English was the lingua franca, accents and ways of expressing themselves made communications difficult.

11. The teams continued to use the frameworks and tools from the week's study and to apply these learnings.

12. By the half-way review, some groups had begun struggling with the project, and with how to work together, how to hold one another accountable, how to use the supportive coaching faculty.

13. At the end of the programme, only half the teams qualified for certification.

But for those who invested the time and effort, they still talk about the project work (not the actual learning process), and how valuable it was.

rated as the most significant part of any program, especially when people are from different businesses, cultures and countries. This is where technology plays a crucial role. People can now learn at their own speed, at a time convenient to them, and at their own workstation. This learning transcends time zones, and can be accessed at any time, almost anywhere today. Mobile-enabled learning (MEL), e-learning, simulations, gaming, webinars and podcasts all play a crucial role in helping you to learn. And making those relevant learnings "stick." Importantly, you can be in any country, and learn while travelling.

I love using my mobile phone to learn about the new products and services our company is developing. Hanging around airports, which I do regularly, means I am learning even when I am standing in line to go through security or board a plane. What is more remarkable is that I can then access the attached web link to see how our customers are using these products, and then synchronize live chat between our R&D and sales teams. On the go and we are all learning from one another. This has helped me enhance my ability to communicate with greater clarity, and to collaborate more effectively with my colleagues in other regions.

— Regional Head of Sales, Africa, for a global telecoms company

For those of you who are used to just sitting in a classroom and listening, often in a passive mode, this is a big change. If you are not yet very comfortable using technology, it might even seem a bit daunting. But practise a few times. You will wonder why you ever thought it would be difficult. It is a golden opportunity to connect with people from all over the world, but also learn from them as well. Using technology, you have the opportunity to be more proactive, ask loads of questions, work in teams to complete projects, as well as connect and collaborate with other participants through blogging and social networking sites. This will help you become a global player as you learn to understand the language of others, how they think, and how they behave.

How about playing?

Gaming is an effective learning tool, since it allows participants to practise real-life simulations. For the generation that grew up with video games, you will no doubt be delighted. For the generation that nagged your kids to stop playing video games, you might be sceptical or even alarmed. Please do persevere. You will be surprised at how much you can learn with this technique. But make sure you are playing recommended and highly regarded games. The Simulation Development Group, for example, has developed a training game that lets you "Live a day as your CEO." Your HR team should be able to assist in recommending suitable games. Top-tier universities, including Harvard and Insead, have recently introduced powerful virtual learning opportunities. Try to join a global group.

Typically, workplace games incorporate a case history of the relevant industry and organization, a set of realistic rules guiding business decisions, and sometimes a computerized mathematical model which simulates a dynamic market. They offer possibilities for experiential learning in strategic planning and policy making, functional integration, financial analysis and control, and team planning. Risk management is learnt through the "what if" analysis and there are also opportunities to enhance interpersonal behavioural training.

Games allow managers to experience failure without personal or organizational consequences. For example, strategizing through playful design is a useful complement to dry, conventional strategic planning processes and helps foster debate about an organization's particular strategic challenges.

In project management most games focus on the planning phase of a project. The focus can be on real business issues, and some of the potential problems, likely to be encountered during the project's execution. Problem solving, decision making and root cause analysis are all brought to the fore. What a better way to improve project managers' techniques and experience in reacting to unexpected events and preparing for the actual execution of a project?

Importantly, by simulating realistic economic and market conditions, the models and concepts learned and solutions generated in a classroom environment can easily be transferred to the real business environment.

Global learning ecosystem

In a world where use of technology is increasing, and collaboration is a must, a range of learning paradigms and training techniques are finding their way into universities, colleges, training centres and learning institutes.

Learning will span national boundaries. Joint ventures and sharing will change the way educational institutions operate in a global learning ecosystem. Take for example the Reims Management School in France, which boasts of adding 13 new schools to its network of global partners, taking it to 150 partner universities in 40 countries. In 2010 it hosts around 900 international students on its campus—certainly an attraction for people who wish to enter the global employment arena.

There will be many more virtual campuses attracting virtual students from everywhere. Most probably, much of our advanced education will be via virtual-learning institutes and universities. You will be learning alongside people from all over the world, but you many never meet them face to face; instead, conference calls, VCs, and blogging will play a greater role in your learning.

Social networking sites, via both intranet and internet, will also be invaluable learning sites for you. But beware, many of these are focused on people looking for jobs or people looking to "sell" something they do. It is best not to spend all your time here, but to look for more academic, or at least more seriously focused discussions.

Your learning future

As the hierarchical structure of learning splinters, traditional top-down movements of authority, knowledge, and power will unravel. Bosses often don't have the experience or information that *you* have been able to access or absorb. In fact many organizations today have upward coaching and mentoring from "young talent" to the big bosses.

At times it may feel as though we are buried beneath an avalanche of information, measures and metrics. We will need

E-LEARNING RESOURCES

Institutes and organizations that have developed innovations to facilitate e-learning:

- **The Kelly Scientific Learning Center** is an interactive online training campus providing career development opportunities for scientific professionals. The centre offers self-paced introductory, intermediate and advanced courses in soft skills (personal development and management) and technical skills (www.kellyscientific.us/web/us/ksr/en/pages/e_learning_career.html).

- **Elearnspace** is site and blog to help you explore e-learning, knowledge management, networks, technology, and community (www.elearnspace.org).

- **St George's University in London e-Learning Unit (ELU)** was established in 2001 to promote the use of educational technology in enhancing learning and teaching across the institution, within the context of St George's teaching and learning strategy. Its other interests are in e-learning strategy, the investigation of emerging technologies, and evaluation of its e-supported learning approaches and techniques (www.elu.sgul.ac.uk/elu/).

to decide which data is relevant and why, and how to abstract the relevant perspectives. One of the precious skills in the information age is the ability to prioritize—this informs how you decide to act upon what you know. We will also need to explore how we can fairly evaluate performance when it often seems that we can't keep up with the email and information overload.

Conceptual and theoretical learning on its own will become less and less relevant. New concepts and new ways of thinking will be needed—but what you learn will need to be applicable to a variety of different job situations. Remember, you are unlikely to have a job for life, and quite likely to work in a variety of locations, with many different people from a variety of different backgrounds.

The Global You will therefore need a broad-based set of transferable behaviours such as empathy, adaptiveness, curiosity, and the ability to transfer knowledge from one role or one job to another, no matter where. Learning is not just doing your MBA, learning is now for life. But learning is not about just absorbing knowledge. It is about knowing where to find information, and to combine that with your experience to build perspective and enhance your ability to make good judgements in a variety of different situations.

Think paradox. Accept ambiguity

The learning needed for the global world involves a blend of cognitive and experiential approaches; global workers typically are able to blend left-brain and right-brain ability. People with a linear, left-brain approach to business, assuming there are discrete causes and effects and a single mode of operating as an international worker, struggle in the flat world. Those who can accept apparent paradox, and be comfortable with ambiguity—both right-brain facilities—are better equipped.

For example, managers who are comfortable with the paradox that international management implies being both empowering to colleagues and closely co-ordinating of activities will thrive. It sounds like a contradiction, but it is not when viewed in terms of teamwork, rather than structure or reporting lines. An effective manager will have powers of empathy, will be a good listener, will try to understand different cultures, and will permit autonomy to those individuals where they have expertise. But he or she will stay well-informed of the activity and performance of different teams. He or she will ensure different elements are supporting one another, will tackle poor performance, and ensure that there is consistency and direction around coherent business goals.

It can be argued that the left brain—specialist, scientific, rational—has been overly dominant in business planning and thinking. This approach is perfectly suited for dealing with clearly defined problem-solving, less good at considering the big picture, or assimilating a rapidly changing context.

There's an increasing amount of research on this. In *The Master and His Emissary: The Divided Brain and the Making of the Western World*, Iain McGilchrist describes how the left and right brains are complementary, but that the left has become overly influential— certainly in Western business culture. Reviewing the work, the moral philosopher Mary Midgley observes that the best way in which the two halves work together is when the right brain perceives the overall picture, prioritizes, and delegates a certain activity to the left brain for analysis. The problems come when the left brain holds on to it for too long, and becomes dismissive of any form of analysis that does not involve measurement:

> Since it is the nature of precision not to look outward—not to bother about what is around it—the specialist partner does not always know when it ought to hand its project back to headquarters for further processing…. Our whole idea of what counts as scientific or professional has shifted towards literal precision— towards elevating quantity over quality and theory over experience.

In the run-up to the credit crisis, investment banks' risk specialists developed highly complex formulae for "calculating" market risk. Faith was placed in the models, and those issuing warnings based on experience and the bigger picture were not listened to.

Every day is another new lesson

As well as work-related learning, effective global workers attend to general education about the world around them. There is a balance to be struck, of course. In periods where the work-load is heavy and the deadlines are pressing, there's little time to read the *Harvard Business Review* or exchange ideas on World Café. But working life— fortunately—does not divide neatly into learning and doing: meeting that deadline *is* the educational opportunity.

In the course of working life, every day is a lesson. Many people say that the world of work is "constantly changing," and sometimes it sounds like a complaint. It raises a question: what is our expectation? That things stay the same? Just how realistic is that, in a world of around six billion highly curious, inventive, sentient beings called humans? If we see all change as a learning opportunity, our perspective alters.

As Barack Obama's adviser Rahm Emanuel famously quipped: "You never want to let a serious crisis go to waste." So even when projects have not gone to plan, there is a learning opportunity. The exercises described earlier in this chapter are focused on maximizing the control you can bring to bear on the learning that you need for a particular challenge—but there are also lessons to learn when the unexpected happens.

The Global You expects every day to bring something new, and welcomes this. When things stay the same, you are disappointed and frustrated. Change is an expectation and an opportunity, not a problem. Globalization and the internet have wrought dramatic changes in the ways in which businesses make money and consumers access information and services. Previously reliable sources of income, where margins were high because certain key players, such as print publishers, estate agents or intermediate purchasers had a fair degree of control over certain media, access to markets or to information, have become much less so. The internet has dramatically lessened the threshold of entry to and eased trading arrangements in certain sectors—especially music, newspaper publishing, and second-hand markets for anything from iPods to luxury apartments. Technology, media and telecoms sectors—previously separate— have merged, as technology firms, for example, look to own content.

Amazon, originally a technology retail outlet, has produced a new format for reading books, the Kindle, and become a publisher through its deal with prominent literary agent Andrew Wylie, who represents Salman Rushdie, Philip Roth and others. It is probable that there will be more such moves out of traditional business areas in media, publishing and music.

In these areas, the businesses and the people who were adaptable, and who learned to learn continuously in the pre-Web 2.0 days, are also the ones most likely to survive and thrive in the new environment. They understand that new media are just means of communication, and the principles of good customer service, good leadership of employees, and good teamwork, are still fundamental to any enterprise.

So, for example, publishers and editors who have grown up in the world of print and display advertising have to learn about webinars, podcasts, YouTube, blogs and Twitter. It's a challenge; but it's also more exciting. Profits may be harder to generate, but they are achieved in a much more fascinating way, enabling closer interaction with readers, and a more global reach. Many people's professional lives have been transformed in the past five years or so with the intensification of social networking and other forms of communication, and in many ways they have been enriched. New skills have been learned, new markets reached, new trade relations and routes established and new languages learned.

One of the biggest myths in management—and you still hear it, from time to time—is that "people hate change." This is not true:

people love change. We are fascinated by innovation, news and gossip. We are inquisitive creatures who are easily bored. What the saying probably refers to is that people don't like having their autonomy taken away, or their career paths torn up. People actually love change; we just want to be part of it, not have it become something that's done to us. This is as true of globalization as it is of any other form of change.

Key to this is to treat every day as a lesson and seek always to grow and develop.

EXERCISE
ACTION LEARNING PLAN
Make your learning stick

Remember: "If nothing concrete happens within 30 days after a session, nothing will ever happen." It is now up to you! So don't be passive about making your learning experiences being put to work. Make your own Action Learning System.

Take a look at the example we have drawn up on the next page, which we've filled in with hypothetical entries to show you how it should be used.

Make a table like that for yourself, and start filling it in. The idea is to really spell out for yourself the concrete steps you will be taking, and the tangible benchmarks by which you will judge your progress and eventual success.

continued >>>

CURRENT ROLE	Vice-President, Procurement (soft furnishings), for a 4-star European hotel chain
CAREER ASPIRATIONS	President, Procurement, for a 5-star global hotel chain
DEVELOPMENT INITIATIVE	Learn to connect better with vendors in China and India
HOW DO I STACK UP?	Last month there was an error in the price I got from an Indian vendor as the local term for 100,000 is a *lakh*, and I misunderstood this.
	Also, the language on the contract was confusing, and thus the order was placed a week late.
WHAT DO I NEED TO LEARN?	I need to get familiar with the terminology used in India so that there are no more errors in procurement.
HOW WILL I DO THIS?	I will start by reading up on these terminologies. I also have a neighbour who is a finance person in another company, and I will ask him if he would mind spending half an hour with me over a cup of coffee to help me get started.
	I am planning a vacation over the summer, and I might plan to go to India. I could then spend a couple of days meeting up with my counterparts there. I doubt if my current company would sponsor a trip to India, but they might for some of it.
HOW WILL I MEASURE MY PROGRESS?	My relationship with my colleagues abroad is stronger. They are more responsive.
	Zero error in purchase orders

6 GO VIRTUAL WHILE STAYING REAL

There is a YouTube video entitled "Social Media Revolution" that, at the point of writing, has been viewed almost 1.25 million times. It has done the rounds of the global marketing tribe and associated professions and created quite a stir. It challenges the notion that social media is a fad (without specifying if this is a common idea), and asks whether it should instead be seen as the biggest change since the Industrial Revolution. It contains some remarkable statistics on the rise of social networking—and the relative decline of traditional media such as newspapers—as conduits for information. Some of the statements are unquestionably true; some are unverifiable, but it is unlikely that any are a long way wide of the mark. Some are surprising; some are to be expected. None can be safely ignored:

- In 2010 Generation Y begins to outnumber Baby Boomers, and 96 per cent will have joined a social network.

- If Facebook were a country, it would be the fourth largest, after China, India and the USA. Yet China's QZone is even larger, with 300 million users.

- Eight out of ten employers use LinkedIn as the primary tool to find employees.

- The fastest-growing demographic on Facebook is women aged 55–65.

- Some 80 per cent of Twitter usage is on mobile devices.

- Generation Y and Z regard email as passé.

- 24 of the 25 largest newspapers are experiencing record declines in circulation.

World wide friends

The first social networking site, SixDegrees, was launched in 1997. Members could find and send messages to friends, and then communicate with each other's friends and family online. In October 2009, more than 830 million users visited social networks via home and office computers (*National Geographic*, March 2010).

So much communication takes place on social networking sites. Not only networking for work, which is now a regular feature of these sites, but also for sharing vacation photos, weddings invitations, birth announcements, and more. Friends and family can connect quickly and frequently in what some find is a slightly more impersonal way than a personal email, and is open and easily accessible anywhere, anytime.

Growth has been rapid, and there is likely to be further growth, as well as diversification of media and forms of interaction, in the next ten years. At the time of writing, Apple's iPad, promising higher-quality range and depth of visual communication, has just been launched, and e-book formats such as Kindle are growing in popularity.

These are two technological wonders for you to think about incorporating into your tool kit. If you love reading the newspaper, but all you find while travelling is a local daily—or you find none at all in your language—reading online solves the problem. Or if you just feel like reading a good book, and you can't find it in a book store, you will similarly be able to buy one online and read it immediately. Whereas if you typically prefer to read a "tree" book, you either have to fit it into your luggage and weight allowance, or need to be able to buy it.

Going virtual

Business-to-business applications of new technology are also growing. Virtual, three-dimensional "second-life" technology is becoming more popular for training. The virtual exhibition, in which the user "visits" three-dimensional stands, is now a reality, with considerable savings for companies in reduced hotel and travel bills. It is possible that in ten years' time the typical visit to a website will convey the sensation of a three-dimensional space, rather than a flat screen dominated by words.

To many people, the facts and developments sketched out above are familiar, but for some there is still a learning curve, and it points upwards:

> I had always had a full-time secretary until the economic meltdown. I am embarrassed to say that she even printed out my emails for me and I would dictate the answers for her. When I was travelling, even though I had a Blackberry, I never bothered answering any email that would be longer than five words. Even that often took me longer than five minutes. When our company downsized and my secretary left the company, I didn't even know where to begin. Glancing around me,

everyone seemed fine doing their own work. I was suffocating under technology. Actually, it only took me about four months to get the hang of things. I swore I would never let that happen to me again.

— Senior banking executive, based in Jakarta

It's important, however, when looking at new technology, to distinguish between genuinely new features, and unchanging verities; accordingly this next section will be sub-divided into two broad categories: What changes, and what stays the same.

What changes

It is common to observe that change, especially in mobile devices and communications technology, occurs at a dizzying pace, and that it is hard to keep up. Whether or not change is rapid depends upon expectations, however. In this respect, the theme of this chapter, multimedia, is close to that of the previous, learning to learn. Those who continually expect change, who are disappointed when it doesn't happen, who are continually "in the classroom," and expect to be learning something new every day, are less taken by surprise by changing media or markets. They will both expect and hope that new ways of communicating with customers or employees will continue to appear, and be eager to seize the opportunities.

Virtual interaction

In the field of medical care, for example, new technology can lead to a deeper understanding and interaction between doctor and patient without taking up much more of the physician's time, and sometimes by reducing the need for a frail individual to travel to hospital. Writing in *Harvard Business Review* (Jan/Feb 2010), Ronald Dixon MD, director of the Virtual Practice Project at Massachusetts General Hospital, observes that he is able to minimize the tiring and disruptive visits to hospital by frail patients through the simple task of making checks via the telephone. He adds:

> *Now imagine that instead of simply having a phone conversation, we could remotely monitor patients using a kiosk like the one some colleagues and I are currently alpha testing. If reliable data on blood pressure, pulse rate, and so forth could be captured and beamed to the physician, some fragile individuals would be saved the necessity of making trips to the doctor's office. And physicians would have many more readings, meaning more chances to discern patterns and detect anomalies in time to act.*

Some clinics in the USA have already introduced ongoing assessments virtually, so that if a patient's pacemaker, for example, is not working properly, immediate interventions can be initiated through a network of clinics all over the world.

In experiments with patients, both video-based consultation and "email visits" produced high levels of satisfaction. Says Dixon, "When the day comes that physicians and patients readily engage in all three types of virtual interaction—asynchronous (such as email), synchronous but remote (video-conferencing) and device-intermediated (kiosk collection of vital signs), up to three-fifths of today's office visits can be eliminated."

Multimedia changes the way we think?

Multi-tasking, constant interruptions, being "always on" in a 24/7 hyper-linked world, would seem to be profoundly affecting how we absorb information and relate to one another. There are some fears that we are losing our capacity to concentrate on longer books or articles, which is necessary for understanding something in depth. For example, it may not be enough to know about China's recent announcements—you might need to research for a report on its trade and investment strategies since the 1970s. For this, you need seriously researched, in-depth study. Are our multi-tasking, subject-skimming, constantly-surfing minds up to the task? The September 2009 edition of *Harvard Business Review*, "Death by Information Overload," reported that research had shown that constant interruption of people's work by email was damaging effective working.

There are certainly dangers here, but it is important to keep ourselves in charge. Skimming different short items and losing the habit of serious study is a choice, an invitation—it's never compulsory. In an eloquent riposte to "Death by Information Overload," Francis Wade, the president of Framework Consulting, wrote:

Information is actually benign. The quantity of information that exists exerts no force of its own, and the same is true of all the information that's flying around the internet. You and you alone decide where to place your attention. If you care that a famous film-maker was just arrested in Switzerland on charges of statutory rape,

it's not because the information is rushing at you. You have selected it
out of the vast library of all the gossip that exists and have decided to
focus on it. But if the information isn't producing the burden, what is?
It must be us, or more accurately, it must be our own habits. There is
nothing inherently burdensome about getting a lot of email, any more
than there is anything inherently burdensome about being a manager.

The early days of the web were about more information—more
was always better. When email first appeared, it was a pleasure
to read messages on a screen and not have to go through piles of
paper correspondence. As the technology has matured and the flow
of information has increased, the task becomes more a matter of
filtering, marshalling and prioritizing that information, looking hard
at the quality, influence and relevance of interactions and media, and
not assuming that more is necessarily best.

An analogy can be drawn with motor transport. In the early
20th century, for those who could afford a car, the sensation was:
"Great! I'm mobile! And there are paved roads that are mostly
empty." As traffic built up, in came traffic lights, rules, speed limits
and regulations; then freeways, intended to speed things, but which
in turn attracted more traffic. So complaining about a surfeit of
information on the Web, when working in a 21st-century business,
is a bit like living in downtown Manhattan and moaning about all
the cars.

When faced with a overabundance of reading material, remind
yourself that journalists are trained to work hard on the headline
and introductory paragraph to draw the reader in; their ultimate

achievement is to lure someone to read a whole item without consciously intending to. The defence mechanism against such wiliness is to train yourself to flip the off-switch, to have the discipline to say: "That story about Tiger Woods does not fall into the prioritized subject area of reading for today; it's not even in the top ten. But I'll bookmark it to read over a cup of tea in the evening."

At times, it's hard to regard reading online news items as "work"—but we do have to stay abreast of developments. The key word is: prioritize. Core subjects first, related subjects second, sports and entertainment third (unless, of course, you work in sports or the theatre, or it is a very important part of your life to have the latest updates!).

What stays the same

Although there is much talk about social networking and Web 2.0 transforming business, much of it is rather breathless, bordering on hype. Vague marketing phraseology referring to "human algorithms" and "social architecture" can erect a barrier to potential new entrants. It gives the misleading impression that we are discussing something other than the straightforward task of communicating with other people about business and services. Ironically, some discussions and blogs intended to advertise the potential of such online interactions leave people feeling overwhelmed or excluded, and deter further involvement.

The smartest entrepreneurs, managers and other workers are those who are not dazzled or fazed by such talk of new paradigms, but who instead identify what has stayed the same.

It is important, firstly, to remember that nothing can replace face-to-face communication from time to time.

When Jamie D. heard of an opportunity to join a tech start-up firm, he jumped at the opportunity. For the past few years he had constantly complained about big-company politics and bureaucracy holding him back, so this was going to be his chance to shine. As president in charge of marketing and fundraising, he was to be based in New York while the founders and tech experts were located in California. He put his heart and soul into the job, focusing on building a new business model and driving revenue. He had initially agreed to attend regular quarterly management and board meetings, but being so task-focused he couldn't be bothered to join the team over dinners or engage in their "stupid" offsite meetings.

A year later he was horrified to find that they had decided to let him go. After all, hadn't he just raised $20 million in the last round? He did have the courage to talk to them when he recognized how he had neglected to build strong relationships with his colleagues. It took a round of face-to-face meetings with all the six founding partners, continuous calls, and a three-day offsite in Miami, for things to start getting better.

Two years later and Jamie has managed to pull off the IPO, and the company is doing really well despite the economic environment. He learnt his lesson the hard way, and now spends at least 25 per cent of his time keeping his networks in shape. And he never misses a board meeting. Importantly, he makes sure he has face-to-face time, either in formal meetings or informally over dinner or a beer, to stay connected.

—— President, technology company, Manhattan

What stays the same in the Web 2.0 world and in the adoption of new media are some elements of human nature: the desire for trust, engagement, meaning and respect. Web 2.0 communication does not lessen their importance; on the contrary it highlights them in new ways. One of the assertions from the YouTube video was that 78 per cent of people trust a peer's recommendation about a product or service, while only 14 per cent trust advertisements. So the upheavals in the advertisement business, causing such disorientation on the part of sales managers globally, especially in traditional print media, actually derive from a sharpened focus on an ancient principle—trust.

Customers are demanding more information, more peer review, more interaction, before buying. Woe betide any company that provides poor quality products or services. Most retailer sites, such as Amazon or Best Buy in the USA, encourage people to write a review and rate the product or service. Some consumers simply start blogs, writing good or lousy reports about their experiences.

Advertisers are hence increasingly reluctant to part with cash for generic display advertisements, and are more likely to pay for ways to approach potential customers directly, to learn their preferences and buying patterns—in short, to focus. It's almost a return to pre-Industrial Revolution times, before the advent of mass communication and advertising, when people would exchange ideas in villages and communities. The modern "village" may be a LinkedIn group, rather than the nearby homes clustered around the church or mosque, but the principle is timeless.

Indeed, the marketing profession's new emphasis on digital tribes—grouping customers around shared interests, rather than social and demographic definitions–is a more commonsense idea than the rather arbitrary demographic groupings of A, B, C1, C2 and so on. Web 2.0 media can, paradoxically, enable a more

---

OLD SPICE SALES DOUBLE WITH YOUTUBE CAMPAIGN

A team of creatives, tech geeks, marketers and writers gathered in an undisclosed location in Portland, Oregon yesterday [13 July 2010] and produced 87 short comedic YouTube videos about Old Spice. In real time. They leveraged Twitter, Facebook, Reddit and blogs.... Everybody loved it; those videos and 74 more made so far today have now been viewed more than 4 million times and counting. www.readwriteweb.com

---

traditional way of bonding with others than was possible in the rather impersonal 20th-century forms of mass communication.

And people still want to meet. Twitter has seen explosive growth in use in the past couple of years online—but it has led to the phenomenon of the real-life "Tweet-up." And while magazine and newspaper publishers struggle to maintain advertising revenues from print and online publishing, they are realising that they can actually make more money from conferences, breakfast briefings, sponsored events, and so on. The oldest form of human interacting—getting together and meeting—is enjoying a resurgence.

Optimize, not maximize, automation

One of the things that some service companies get spectacularly wrong in Web 2.0 is to over-automate; to fail to select the right medium for the message. Nowhere is this more evident than in customer service.

Many call centres think that they are saving themselves costs by putting formidable electronic barriers between the customer and the service, forcing people to spend minutes or even hours going through layer after layer of automated options, some of which are patronizing, built around sets of multiple-choice questions designed to tease out which stupid mistake the customer has made.

Some companies have begun making the apparently retrograde step of re-inserting a telephone number on their home pages. This is not a retreat from Web 2.0. On the contrary, it's a recognition that service always comes first, and that there are some situations which the designers of the automated help programmes had simply not thought of.

In the same way, conventional conferences, offsites and meetings have not gone out of fashion; they remain essential for socializing and deeper getting-to-know-you. In fact, now that the world economy seems to be stabilizing, more and more teams are organizing these work "get-togethers," pulling people together from several geographies.

Good protocol

The basic protocols of courtesy and respect for human dignity apply online, just as much as anywhere else. It is possible to shout at or nag other people virtually. Constantly advertising your abilities and promoting yourself via updates on Twitter or Facebook can start to bother people, just as much as if you dominated the conversation at a lunch meeting, talking only about yourself. It is courteous to show a genuine interest in the goals and motivations of other people, as well as advertising your own.

Empathy is just as important in online communications as in face-to-face meetings, and it takes greater effort without the visual cues of body language. The principles of colleague relations and customer service are timeless. You can engage, please and delight people through any medium. You can also insult, harass and annoy. You can assert your rights, or you can let people walk all over you, just as much as in a meeting. In a virtual meeting it is just that much more complex.

Optimal use applies to social media by individuals, as well as automation by companies. You don't have to be on all the different social media networks; and it is positively harmful for such an activity to completely replace conventional conversations, meetings and phone calls. It's probably best to make use of a core set of, say, four or five social networks, and share links intensively between them, than try to maintain active presence on 20 or 30. Activity does not guarantee influence.

Intranet or outranet?

If you are a working for a small company, or indeed run a smallish business, or are an independent consultant trader, you will find that using technology to connect with affiliates, or other sole traders with whom you are working, is the best way to connect. Whether people are in meetings or on the job and unable to take your call, they are likely to catch up with you a few hours later to discuss work issues and opportunities. Subcontracting to people who do not work in the same organization as you is the shape of most organizations today, whether it is for infrastructure services, catering, cleaning, nursing, customer call centres or security. When working across time zones it becomes a daily matter of course.

In-house blogging and knowledge management are all on the intranet, but of course, not available to the public. So for building your external networks you could join some "outranet" blogging applications, where membership is controlled or limited, for example, to folks who have attended a particular executive education program, or, say, an association of the many boatbuilders across the country. This is the mission statement of the American Boatbuilders Association:

> Through the collective buying power of its members, we will strive to purchase high quality materials at the lowest cost of any boat building entity in the United States. We will organize as necessary to bring the united voice of the independent builder to outside influences such as suppliers, government, and industry associations.

Now take a moment to think as to how positively this can impact customers, and how helpful this "outranet" is to the boatbuilders.

The future is here to stay

Being tech-savvy is no longer an optional skill today. Whether you are booking your travel, paying a bill, or making a reservation at a restaurant, you now have the choice of hanging on the phone for ages, speaking to an automated voice system, or taking only a few minutes to make a transaction online. Activities like "going to your bank to pay a bill or set up an account" or organizing a vacation by "visiting" a travel agent are disappearing. It can all be done online or by phone. Viewing the villa you want to rent in the Maldives, or sorting out a trip to the Galapagos, becomes an easy transaction. Soon, some of the "older" options will disappear entirely, and you will only be able to check things out on your mobile or PC.

You may think that projections towards a mobile device-centred economy are far-fetched, but travelling to almost every country today, one cannot help but notice how much time people spend on their mobiles, not only talking, but texting, going online, or connecting to a website. Strangely enough, in many so-called "underdeveloped" countries, mobile phones have leapfrogged over landlines and cables, and everyday folk there are far more technologically progressive than in the West. It is not unusual in many remote, rural parts of Africa and Asia for people who have had no access to schooling, and often from low socio-economic strata, to conduct all their business using technology.

VIRTUAL SHAKESPEARE THEATRE? DON'T BE ABSURD!

Who would have thought that Shakespeare's *Romeo and Juliet* would have a 21st-century makeover on Twitter, one of the most powerful and influential social networking sites, in existence since just 2007?

"Such Tweet Sorrow" premiered in April 2010 under the auspices of the world-famous—and very traditional— Royal Shakespeare Company. Over a five-week period, the actors improvised around a prepared story "grid," set in modern-day Britain rather than olden-day Italy, responding to one another, to the "audience," and to real-world events. Believe it or not the actors wrote the tweets themselves, guided by the storyline and diary which outlined where they were at any moment in the adventure. RSC actress Charlotte Wakefield played the 16-year-old Juliet, tweeting her daily activities under the Twitter name "julietcap16." She even linked a YouTube video of her bedroom— pausing on a framed photo of her dead mother.

This experimental Twitter drama was co-produced by Mudlark, a company which produces entertainment on mobile phones. Their mission was to connect people with Shakespeare and bring actors and audiences closer together: "Mobile phones don't need to be the antichrist for theatre. This digital experiment... allows

continued >>>

our actors to use mobiles to tell their stories in real time and reach people wherever they are in a global theatre."

Now, if they can do virtual theatre, you need to be able to enjoy it. So if you are not comfortable with the technology, you will be left out.

And what about organizations? Can they use "virtual industrial theatre" for large sales meets, workshops and global dialogues? Imagine the engagement of team members if the integration of a merger or acquisition was enhanced using virtual industrial theatre? Or if a new product or service was being introduced that way. As visual communication would transcend cultural and language barriers, the impact via mobile phone could be riveting. The impact of any strategic decision would be dramatically enhanced. Why then are organizations lagging behind?

No wonder that most Apple stores are buzzing with customers; and now that the iPad has been launched, many of the stores in the USA feel more like bustling markets, rather than expensive boutiques.

The new applications, gadgets, widgets, gizmos that are born constantly are unending. Whether you are paying a bill, learning about a new product or service your company is planning to introduce, picking up a webinar or podcast, or simply texting your kids, the internet-enabled mobile phone

TIPS FOR OPERATING IN MULTIMEDIA

1. If you have teenage kids or know teenagers of friends or neighbours, spend an hour with them for an update lesson at least once a month.

2. Draw up a lesson plan for yourself, especially of "what you don't know you don't know." Many lessons and instructions can be downloaded from the internet.

3. If you buy a Mac in the US, for an extra $100 you can have any number of one-on-one lessons over 12 months. Apple's home page lists a number of free tutorials, and is a good place to start becoming an expert user. www.apple.com/startpage

4. Once a month, pop into a bookstore to pick up any technology magazine. Read the reviews of existing applications and keep up to date with what new ones are forthcoming.

5. For the latest in mobile-phone technology, the internet will let you know all the news and views. findarticles.com/p/articles/mi_m3457/

is definitely where the future of technology—at least over the next few years, until something else comes on the market—lies. So wherever you are and whatever you are doing, make sure you don't get left behind.

7 TREAT MULTI-CULTURAL TEAMWORK AS A CORE SKILL

After reading the previous chapter, you may think that if you have mastered the latest technology, teamwork is not really that important anymore. Emails, "webinars" and tele-conferences seem to be working well, without you having to bother much with what is going on at the receiving end. Moreover, in the view of many managers in global businesses today, English is the medium almost everywhere, basic communication is enough; and as the team is widely dispersed it is probably impossible to work as a team anyway. Teams can start to look like a dispensable option.

The economic downturn stopped almost all unessential business travel. Team-building meetings and workshops were unheard of during that period. And you know what, things kept ticking over quite well without worrying about all that multi-cultural stuff. We had no choice. Now that business is picking up, I plan to organize a meeting of our ten regional sales managers. I woke up this morning realizing I haven't got a clue how to start. One of the team suggested we meet in Dubai as a central location, but another told me he felt slighted that we were not meeting in Tokyo. The turf wars have already started.... Can you help?

—Head of sales of an international telecoms company, currently based in Qatar, making this comment in April 2010

> I don't see why we even meet as a team when we have nothing in common. Anyway they still, after all this time, regard themselves superior to us.
>
> **—Local manager in South Africa mining, who was extremely irritated when the British bosses organized six monthly team workshops**

But even if people who are working together on a project rarely or never get to meet, they are still a team. There is little or nothing you can do on your own. There is much frustration and wasted effort if your colleagues do not know one another's roles, or simply do not know one another. So where should you start?

Do you have the right people on the bus? The basics

If you are the leader of a multi-cultural team it is important to appoint people who are not only great at their jobs, but who also have global mindsets and cross-cultural, cross-border ways of feeling as well as thinking. If you are a team member, these are some of the areas you will need to assess yourself. Remember, being a Global You starts with the basics, but these basics need constant nurturing to continue to grow and develop. So in essence what does this mean?

Think big and be open

First, the Global You should have the ability to influence and inspire the thinking, attitudes and behaviour of people from all over the world (Adler 2001; Dorfman 2003). As structures get flatter and less hierarchical, this ability should be a core competence for all team members, not just the team leader. It is about motivating colleagues and suppliers, government officials and agencies, and other stakeholders. For example if you are part of the procurement team for a food retailer in Europe, you may need to influence farmers or co-operatives in Kenya, or Chile, to supply you with their produce.

To be open means that you will be interested in working and even living abroad. Even though you may still appreciate and love your own country, or culture, or religion best, you will need to gain a broader view of the global world, and be able to reflect out of your own national worldview. Worldwide business thinking should start to be natural to you. For example, many Western businesses saw China and India mainly as manufacturing and outsourcing hubs. It was only the economic downturn which helped many managers to start viewing these countries as huge customer and consumer hubs. Some, like P&G and Siemens, had a jump start with an already existing market.

Yes, the leopard can change its spots

Learn to acquire new beliefs about people who are different from you, and to re-evaluate these worldviews as you expand your frame of reference. If you are a team leader, it will involve asking people about their thoughts, opinions and ideas about particular cultures, and importantly, first-hand observation as to how they behave with "others." If something surprises you about someone's behaviour—for example, they are late for meetings, or quiet during them—find out why; don't assume it's a disciplinary matter or a problem; it might just be a different cultural lens.

Global team leaders will also need to adapt different leadership styles in order to lead, inspire, and influence people from different cultures. For example, in some countries, say the Netherlands, using a strong democratic style might work best. In some Asian countries, such as Japan and Thailand, a more visionary and directive approach, at least initially, will probably create more engagement. In some cultures people might be reluctant, for a while, to share their opinions or disagree, if it is typically not part of their way of behaving. Formality and informality also vary greatly. In India, for example, it is quite common to speak to bosses in a formal manner, addressing them as "Mr," "Sir," or "Madam." In London, on the other hand, most people are on a first-name basis. Make sure that you and all the team are sensitive to people from other cultures.

> It was a real shocker for me to see how much time people take off from work in India for events that in the West we would never dream of. For example, it could be for "my mother-in-law's sister's cousin's wedding" or "the funeral of my cousin's work colleague." Only then did I realize how closely Indian families were intertwined. . . . And I thought I came from a close Italian family!
>
> —Italian engineer, working in Delhi

Go on, be there

Although reading about other countries and keeping up to date with news events is a good start to cultivating the Global You, nothing can replace personal experience, not even cross-cultural training programs. Travel as much as you can, and try to live like a local. This will give your incipient global mindset an added depth and breadth that will stand you in good stead when working in a multi-cultural team.

Getting on, getting there

Once you have selected your multi-cultural team it is important to ensure that everyone gets on more or less ok. You will, as a manager, need to continually spend time and energy to ensure that mindsets continue to expand. Team norms or behaviour need to be agreed on and adhered to. The job is never done.

Having just moved to the USA, I am learning that each state has different laws and lifestyles. For example, if a lawyer moves from one state to another, she would have to retake examinations in that state. Taxation is different too. In addition, moving residence to another state demands retaking one's driving licence. Religious focus too, varies from town to town. For example, Boston is predominantly Catholic, and church attendance much higher than in Seattle. The food in Texas is distinctly different from that in Palo Alto. I have been a regular visitor for years, and knew there were some differences between states. But actually living there has really opened my eyes as to how complex this country really is.

—Swedish executive from a
furniture manufacturing company

A GLOBAL MINDSET

Years of research carried out by Professor Mansour Javidan at Thunderbird University, USA, highlights three core areas to assess the competencies of a Global You:

- **Intellectual:** Knowledge and understanding of global business, global markets, global supply chains and socio-political systems
- **Societal:** Trusting relationships with people who are different from themselves
- **Psychological:** Openness, flexibility, respect for and the willingness to work with other cultures

It is well worth doing the Global Mindset Inventory, or ensuring that your team does if you are managing a global team. You can find this on the Thunderbird University website.

If you can, insist that the team meet face-to-face at least at the start of your project or assignment. This will give everyone some time to get to know one another, and is the critical time during which you define how your team is going to work together. There could be a number of steps to follow in your first team meeting, many of which will need to be revisited at regular intervals, even if virtually:

Clarity of the team's objectives

Initially, you will have to define these, but it is also worthwhile taking the time to encourage debate and getting team members engaged so that that are indeed aligned to the common objectives. The goals are hard to meet if, during the coffee break, or in the washroom, people are whispering how impossible or stupid these goals are. Get these concerns, anxieties and suggestions out on the table, rather than leave them dancing silently in the room, hoping that they will just go away....

Keeping track

Take time to facilitate a discussion about the business goals, then the teams' goals. This includes interdependent goals, e.g. common goals of the finance and marketing teams, as well as goals of the finance team only. Everyone should share their own personal objectives with the team, and the interdependent goals between different functions should also be transparent. For example, the HR team would agree to work together with the operations team to reduce attrition rates by two per cent over a three month period. Importantly, all goals, whether performance- or business-related should be tangible and measurable.

Agree on the decision-making procedures, roles and problem-solving mechanisms. Ensure the standard operating procedures are aligned and that all processes are clear.

These sessions must focus on ground rules and how the team will operate. To kick it off, ask each team member to table at least three values that are important to him or her. For example: respect for others, integrity, sticking to commitments. After debate, have

THE LONG-DISTANCE MEETING

A long-distance meeting requires very different preparation from a face-to-face meeting for a successful outcome:

- Ensure that your equipment is working and up to date. You do not want your meeting to be dogged by technological hiccups, such as unclear image or sound, especially if you already have to contend with call "drops" or poor quality lines.

- Always prepare an agenda for the meeting and circulate it upfront. This way no one will feel ignored, even if they are on the other side of the world. If the meeting is scheduled by someone else, it is perfectly OK to request the agenda.

- Listen hard. In a meeting where people are physically present, you will be able to read facial movements and body language. In a long-distance meeting, this is harder to do. Problems of accent and language variance are also exacerbated.

- When unsure, don't be shy to ask someone to repeat what they said: "I couldn't quite hear you (rather

continued >>>

than "get" you), would you mind repeating that again, please?"

- Confirm that you did really understand a message, by asking "What I understood is that you wish to...."

- At the end of the meeting, try to get agreement as to the meeting outcomes and actionables so that these can be emailed to all concerned.

the team choose five out of those tabled that they believe are the most important. Finally, discuss those behaviours and actions that demonstrate each of these values, and clarify those behaviours that could destroy them. Walking the talk is critical for any team, and especially so in a multi-cultural team, because different behaviours are interpreted in different ways.

Plan ahead for subsequent meetings. A lot of people in traditional offices complain of meeting overload; but it is possible to have too few meetings, especially in dispersed teams. The main problem here is a straightforward lack of communication. What often works best is the weekly meeting, for people at the same location, or weekly tele-conference, for dispersed teams. These can be quite short, if people come prepared, and outputs are clarified up front. If you are located in different regions of the world, it helps if there is a face-to-face at least yearly or twice-yearly.

What happens when we disagree?

A few years ago, the British music industry producer Nick Lowe reminisced in a radio interview about his time managing the rock band Elvis Costello & The Attractions. Commenting on the musicians' frequent arguments, he observed that he never objected. Indeed, he often provoked them. His view was that groups in which the members were nice to one another all the time produced bland music, not anything that was original and made the audience sit up and take notice.

This sounds like typical rock-and-roll rebel talk, but it gains unlikely support from the pages of the august *Harvard Business Review*. In the December 2009 edition, the feature "How to Pick a Good Fight" identified the ability to disagree openly as being key to successful teamwork. Too much harmony and alignment can stultify debate, suppress discussion of business risk and encourage complacency. The article chronicled, for example, how the culture of the investment bank Lehman Brothers had become "too agreeable, too loyal" in the mid-2000s. The people were aligned and supportive of one another, but heading in an extremely high-risk direction. The problem with too much harmony was that no one wanted to blow the whistle and point to the proximity of the cliff-top. The atmosphere discouraged the dissent necessary for a proper exploration of risk through scenario planning and other forms of open discussion. This culture is one of the reasons for Lehman's sudden death.

By contrast, the authors related the case of Rolf Classon, an incoming CEO at a health care company, who was concerned over the risks of a potential major acquisition. With the support of the business owners he arranged a succession of debates on the plan. Crucially, he ensured that the executive who had championed the take-over was given a full voice in the debate, and access to the board. Although the individual concerned was unhappy at the turn of events, his contribution enabled a robust and open exploration of all options for the company, and resulted in a better strategic direction for the company.

Given our individual native intelligence and autonomy as human beings, it is neither realistic nor democratic to assume that we can or should all think alike. That is not what real teamwork consists of. The much sought-after goal of "alignment" of an organization's people with the commercial goals can be misunderstood here. It is, after all, rather unnatural that while we would never tolerate lack of a voice or lack of debate in the social and political setting, we assume it can work within a corporation.

A key part of becoming a global worker is the ability to accept differences, and to debate honestly held differences without resorting to making personal insults or to demonizing the worldviews of those with whom you disagree. But if you do lead a global team, be careful. In Asia, as a generalization, it is considered extremely disrespectful to disagree with the boss, especially when there are other people in the room. It is also an extremely difficult behavior to change overnight.

Disagreement is most creative when there are at least some rules, covering minimum standards of conduct. Too many rules and it kills creativity, common sense, and the exchange of ideas; too few rules and discord will paralyse the team. What matters is getting the balance right—aligning the team, but tolerating dissent. For this to be honest and creative, it means creating a structure and ways of working that enable free discussion.

Plan like a lawyer, implement like a friend

A useful mantra is to "plan like a lawyer, implement like a friend." Used properly, written rules—by clearly setting out jointly agreed values, principles, and expectations—reinforce trust and informal ways of working.

This can be of particular importance in multi-national teams, communicating in English, where only some of the participants are native English speakers. Drafting a set of rules and expectations identifies upfront any potential areas of disagreement—for example, which department or company picks up which costs—and creates a framework for discussing disagreements. Remember, lack of clarity around the road map will cause teams to fumble and stumble.

For formal contractual arrangements, such as an outsourcing deal, a written service level agreement is essential. For more informal teams, the "rules" may be more in the shape of agreed values and principles. The rules should be a means to an end: assisting the creation of trust and teamwork.

Rules become stifling, however, when they become a substitute for decision-making, when a fearful group simply follows what is permitted, rather than explore what can be achieved. They should be seen as providing a foundation for agreement, exchange of ideas and progress, a minimum set of standards below which conduct should not be allowed to fall, but not a ceiling on the group's aspirations. There has to be permission for a "good idea" that hasn't been thought of before.

The multi-cultural dimensions

Every CEO will tell you that a diverse, multi-cultural team is critical in multi-national business. Often they are not sure exactly why, but there is a strong belief that there is a need to connect with customers and vendors using staff members from the same culture as them. Diverse teams are seen as fostering innovation and adding a richness to planning, decision-making and problem-solving. Even in an ideal world, creating and maintaining a multi-cultural team is a formidable challenge that requires commitment and continual communication. Simply putting the team together achieves little.

> *It was clear that even though there were some very good technical people in the team, we were so stuck in our belief that we were the first-class citizens in the team that our acquisition in Spain did not realize the performance we anticipated. Our arrogance, that as the acquirers we were better than them, distanced the locals, making team working very difficult.*
>
> —Team member of an automobile manufacturing company, with HQ in Germany

If you are a member, or about to become a member, of a multi-cultural team, or if you simply work with people from other cultures, here are some essential tips for handling the complexities of multi-cultural working.

Learn to listen well... to feelings as well as content

Give others the chance to communicate their views. Try inquiry if you don't understand or don't agree with them. This, rather than simply disagreeing, will show respect and courtesy. You never know, they may have expressed themselves in ways which were difficult for you to understand. This is especially the case in multi-cultural teams, as reading body language from other cultures is quite difficult. Westerners in particular find it difficult to understand what some Asians are trying to say.

Try to hear what they are really trying to say, as well as listening to the logical content of what they are saying. Intention underpins all.

Help others fit in

Develop an understanding of different religions and cultures. Regardless of background, all colleagues should be treated fairly and inclusively.

> *Day One of the offsite meeting had gone really well. In the evening over dinner, the predominantly male British contingent steered the conversation to cricket. This was fine for the Australian guy, but it left three of us out of ten out in the cold. I am from Moscow, and my other colleague was from New York, and there was a lady from Bangkok. Day Two didn't go quite so well. The three of us were really peeved by their behaviour.*

> — CFO of a bank striving to be global
> but still dominated by the British

Jokes are not funny

Ethnic jokes or snipes are not trivial. "Van der Merwe" jokes in South Africa, Irish or Jewish jokes, gender sayings, jibes about lady drivers or mothers-in-law—all are likely to seriously upset others. Jokes are best left to the owning party, to tell them if they wish.

Even jokes about current affairs can be risky, if you don't know each other well. Take, for example, the following dialogue between an Argentinian and a Chilean during the collapse of the austral currency in Argentina in the 1990s:

"No, I wouldn't do that—not even if you gave me one million australes."

"Yes—that's about five pesos, isn't it?"

If this is between two good friends with few money worries, it can be laughed away. If someone is worrying about her elderly parents losing their life savings, it can cause upset.

Respect and courtesy apply to all

We might think we are being respectful, but others might think we are being discourteous. Try to understand what certain words or behaviours mean in different cultures.

Consider this scene: A polite receptionist in an Indian company, wishing to inform a manager that she had a visitor in reception, told her, "There is a foreigner here to see you." Overhearing this, the visitor, who happened to be a key customer from Manchester, almost walked out.

8 BUILD YOUR PERSONAL NETWORK

One of Barack Obama's favourite books is the historical *Team of Rivals*—"He talks about it all the time," a top aide told *Time* magazine in 2008. Written by Doris Kearns Goodwin, it covers the political life of Abraham Lincoln and his contemporaries before and during the US Civil War, 1861–65. This phrase, "team of rivals," is now being applied to Obama's own cabinet, and is a live term in Washington circles.

Lincoln had an uncanny ability to network. Unlike his rivals, he never let personal grudges develop or fester; he even appointed to his cabinet an individual who had humiliated him years earlier. This grew into a close and highly effective working relationship. When cabinet members argued, he sought to understand their positions and find an ingenious "third way." If he demoted or overruled someone, he ensured they were spared public embarrassment, and went out of his way to check how they were feeling. In this way, he generated loyalty and strong bonds that lasted decades.

Barack Obama's own personal mission is to build strong bonds with influential politicians and business people all over the world. He, too, is seen as willing to embrace a global network. Don't forget he was the first Web 2.0 president, harnessing the power of online social networking sites such as Facebook and Twitter to help him rise to the top of the political tree. By incorporating technology into the lessons of effective operators from the past, Obama has proved himself shrewd enough to embrace modern methods *and* timeless principles, to meet today's challenges.

A strong network of people who support you—to be effective in your work, and build well-being in your life—will drive your engine of effective performance. This is true for global operators at all levels, not just those in senior roles.

Modern working means working in teams. There is less and less that can be done individually. In addition to the project or work-related team efforts, your own career is constructed around a wider network. Nurturing and understanding this network is essential.

Your job is your social balance

We talk about the "work–life balance" as though work were separate from life, not a part of it. Remember, the Gallup World Poll referred to in Chapter 1 noted that the single unifying factor for the world's population was the desire for a good job. This reminds us that your most important asset is your career, not, as politicians in many countries claim, your house. "Work" and "life" are therefore continuous parts of the human experience.

The overlap is becoming bigger as mobile technology allows more work to be done from home, from the airport and from the train. This places extra pressure on us, if we assume that we have to be on duty 24/7. It also means that "social" and "work" networks of friends and contacts naturally overlap—and for many of us, the overlaps are growing. For global workers this has become a way of life. You've taken an assignment in another country, or you've gone for that promotion even though it means a relocation, because your career really matters to you, and you love to learn.

Some people try to draw lines between work and social relationships, for instance using Facebook for social, personal matters, and LinkedIn for work. For most people, however, the lines are blurred. There will always be people you work with who become friends, or vice versa. These develop into formal as well as informal roles and relationships. Most of the forms of communication that any active, inquiring individual is likely to become involved in simply cannot be neatly categorized.

Let's say you are a software developer at a major software house and you are interested in developing and designing websites. This is partly as a potential career option, but partly out of pure interest. So, is the social networking interest group on website design that you join, and in which you engage in long discussions with other members, a work activity, a social one, or a hobby? In all likelihood, it's all three. And that's fine. Even if it doesn't directly inform your work with the proprietary software you deal with in your day job, it's likely to be of some benefit to your employer that you are enhancing your knowledge of the web and your relationships with web developers. It will benefit your career, especially over the longer term; it's intellectually stimulating in its own right; and it's a way of connecting socially with other people, including people from other parts of the world. But, it doesn't take priority over a pressing request from a corporate client of your employer.

This is all common sense, but common sense can be a victim when corporate rules try to limit "unauthorized web use," for example, without being able to define with clarity where work ends and wider social curiosity begins. So even common sense needs constant attention and definition.

Smooth networking

More importantly—and this is only beginning to be appreciated in the globalized world of myriad outsourcing relationships, joint ventures and temporary project teams—the ability to lead, facilitate or just be a part of a team is a valuable skill in itself. The reason it is only being appreciated now is that it doesn't show up in company balance sheets, and is difficult even to represent on a conventional CV.

> It suddenly hit me that the best team I worked in was just like the jazz band I played in on Saturday nights. People would join the team, for a shorter or longer period depending on the project, and then leave, sometimes coming back. Our leader always made it work, by being open, a great listener, and helping newcomers "hit the deck running." If you watched our gig, sometimes an extra trombone or guitar would slide in and play along with us and then disappear for a few hours. Every now and again someone we knew would pick up the mike and sing. The point is, both in music and at work, we had built strong networks, and knew who would work well with us.
>
> — Manager from the international project management company, Bechtel, who has worked in California, Egypt, Nigeria, and now works in Mumbai

The myth that a career is a solo activity must be debunked. Just as a presidency is in effect teamwork, even where it consists of a "team of rivals," the same is true of all roles in global businesses.

Arguably, the teaching of management, being heavily influenced by the rugged individualism of North American culture, has overly emphasized the individual, for example in the thousands of books on leadership skills. Of course, the individual manager or leader does need personal skills, but the individual always works within networks, and works most effectively by harnessing the power of the networks. Consultant and writer Kathleen Paris, of the University of Wisconsin, comments in her book, *The Clover Practice*, "Our popular American heroes—the Lone Ranger, John Wayne, Rambo, Dirty Harry [etc]—are figures that act on their own and succeed on their own ... But to think that we succeed in an organization on our own merit and effort alone is mostly a delusion."

She challenges this concept of solo heroes, setting out three principles for effective working:

1. Tell the truth, always.

2. Speak for yourself (don't presume to speak for others).

3. Declare your interdependence.

She suggests that we think more systematically about the others on whom we depend to get our work completed: "I wonder what we would do differently if we really appreciated the fact that our success depends on other people doing their work well."

You never know who is watching you

We've all seen people damaging their own careers by being hyper-competitive. They see everyone as a potential enemy or rival; trust is almost non-existent. Ironically, for such over-ambitious individuals, their progress gets stalled. For you to succeed, it's likely that others have to succeed too. And not only in your team, but perhaps in a key supplier or joint-venture partner.

Of course rivalry and competition also exist, and that's vital for organizations and the economy. But the deep level of co-operation required, particularly in the service economy and when developing highly sophisticated goods or services, tends still to be under-appreciated.

As your career progresses, so will the careers of key players in your network. And this is something to encourage. In the next chapter, when we introduce the concept of the personal profile, we'll show you how the "Brand Called You" represents a network of individuals in which there is mutual support, as well as competition.

Networks reinforce one another

In the same way that there can be competition and co-operation between individuals, the same is true of networks. At times, the

I heard this guy on his mobile phone in the lobby of the building, shouting at his secretary, using really foul language. He was oblivious to everyone who was walking by. I had no idea then that he was a candidate for the CEO position of one of our clients. I gave this feedback to the partner in question who was handling the search. He wasn't shortlisted as a result.

—Receptionist at a prestigious head-hunting firm in Paris

demands of your various networks—work and social—will appear to be in conflict. However, there are ways you can utilize the expertise in one network to help solve a problem in another.

View your networks not simply as acquaintances and colleagues, but also as sources of insight, learning, expertise and assistance. Say you are in a project team that is collaborating across different organizations—maybe developing standards within a profession. You are about to begin a long meeting or "webinar" related to this project when your line manager suddenly calls you to make an urgent inquiry: Could you source a specialist, or find out about data protection rules in India? You could, of course, curse the conflicting demands; but on the other hand, it may be that people in the meeting you're about to enter could help you with your manager's request. Why not ask an open question at the end: Can anyone help me with this? Most people are keen to demonstrate their knowledge and to help if they can.

To be able to ask a favour like this, though, relies on having nurtured and maintained good relationships throughout your varied networks.

If you get to know people as people, you will discover hidden talents and areas of interest. Just as it's a mistake to stereotype people by nationality or region, it's also not helpful to categorize people too rigidly by profession. The civil engineer you're about to meet might have a lot of knowledge on those "soft" interpersonal leadership skills or have a wealth of expertise on supply chain logistics. You never know until you ask!

EXERCISE
BUILD YOUR NET-VIEW

Take a moment to think about important leaders who introduced positive change in the lives of others. Mahatma Ghandi and Nelson Mandela all worked with strong networks, no matter how difficult the challenge, and how cut off from the world they were. Imagine being incarcerated, with almost no connection to the outside world, for years and even decades and yet still achieving what they did. Take a few minutes to reflect on how they did it. Watch a documentary on how Ghandi marched around India with hordes of followers. How did they know where he was and where he was going?

Now think which people in your life and company have worked well through strong networks. It could be your boss, a direct report, a colleague or a customer. Take a few minutes to understand why it is adding value to their lives and work.

Now, draw a representation of the work-related and social networks that you inhabit; then think of the closeness and importance of each connection in your network. Reflect on where your network is supporting you, and where you might need to tap into. This your "Net-View." It's represented in two dimensions, but it helps to think in three: about the strength and nature of relationships, as well as the number and the category. Is this web borderless?

continued >>>

The purpose of the Net-View is to show the key individuals in your network who will help you achieve what you need to achieve at work. It's best to include all colleagues, partners, suppliers, friends, etc., as in the real world you will have to manage all of them well to be effective. This personal network will probably differ markedly from the formal reporting lines.

Inside the inner circle are people whose relationships are "essential"; those further away are "useful." Use different line styles or colours to denote the different relationships you have with others in your network. For example, we've used solid lines, dotted lines and wavy lines; you could use different colours too.

This is just a suggested diagram – any similar visual representation may work well, if it succeeds in drawing attention to the core relationships that make you and your team or teams work effectively.

Review the networks where you are a member. Are they the right ones? Or have you been too lazy to disconnect yourself from them?

Now table the "value added" from each network, or people in that network. How much time are you spending with them? What are those interdependencies? Why does it work for you or them? Is it for fun or work or both? Then do a network tidy-up, and organize yourself for fun and for work, and check the overlaps. Make sure there are some there.

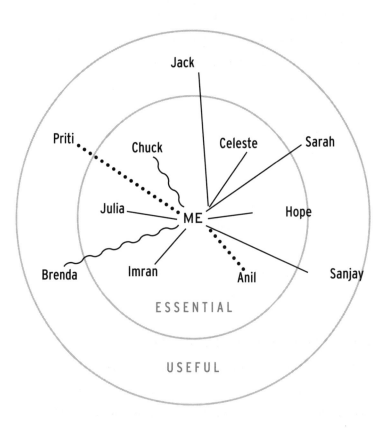

9 RAISE YOUR GLOBAL PROFILE

Whether you are in school, at the start of your career or already established in an organization, you can be sure about one thing—you will be asked about *you*. Either to put yourself on paper, to describe yourself verbally at a formal or informal interview, or to present your one-minute elevator speech.

To succeed globally, you need to have a strong profile, but building your personal profile is much more than simply a question of developing individual promotional material and being on the relevant internet sites, such as Twitter and Facebook. These activities, while important, only form part of what is better conceived as a three-dimensional management of relationships. Building your personal profile is not something you do *to* others, but something you create through interactions *with* others.

Introduce people to one another

In our book, *How to Manage in a Flat World*, we introduced the concept of a "human internet," to describe how enterprises essentially consist of myriads of inter-relationships between people and teams. The most effective global players pay attention to their relationship-building skills; these are seen as a core ability, not as "soft" stuff or a side issue.

Importantly, the best networkers don't just promote themselves, they build relationships with people that they get on with. They put folks in touch with one another who they think would get on. When you do this, think about other people's needs more than your own: will they really want to get to know this person, or are you just

I went to Mumbai knowing one person, my future boss. A client had given me the name of his brother who lived there, and a friend of mine in South Africa had given me the name of a person I could contact which had been given to her by her neighbour. I know it sounds crazy, but believe it or not those two people, out of more than 22 million in the city, knew one another in a work context. One was a journalist for the tourist industry in one of the daily papers, and the other a senior executive in a travel agency. They had met playing tennis initially, as they were members of the same club. Both parties benefited from this friendship—the journalist from always getting a good story, and the travel agency from excellent, free publicity.

—Consultant, previously from Hong Kong,
who had been offered a job in India

I travel and move around a lot for my work, so I make dedicated time to connect with my good friends and close family no matter where I am. Skype is cheap, but there are other deals like pingo and international calling cards. If you are using your mobile it is really cheap. In particular I love instant messenger, for regular on-going contact, at least half a dozen times a day, with my boyfriend, so we know what we are all up to. Great technology today means no excuse for not staying in touch. Now I never feel lonely.... Someone is always connecting at some other time of the day, from another part of the world.

—Consultant with an international strategic
consulting company, based in São Paulo

promoting yourself as someone who's well-connected? If it does turn out to be a mutually useful contact, they'll both thank you for the introduction. This is in keeping with the principle that your profile and your work depend upon a network of relationships, as much as upon individual attainment. A culture of recommending people to people benefits all those involved; and being recommended is the most valuable route to work and promotion.

But don't be too calculating; it's counter-productive to expect an immediate pay-back. Business should be fun and sociable as well as a source of profit and achievement.

Do me a favour

A profile is not just a matter of publicizing your work-based achievements and online publishing. It's more accurate to think of it as the sum of our relationships. This way, we begin to understand our profile in the business world in a more three-dimensional way—how *strong* our relationships are, as well as how *many* there are.

Neither is a profile about a narrow calculation on what favours you owe to someone, or what favour you think someone owes you. It should be a genuine working relationship, with you being free to request information or assistance, and vice versa, with no payback.

What constitutes a favour anyway? Favours and mutual expectations are heavily influenced by culture. For example, if you are new to a country and your business host treats you to what feels like lavish dining and entertaining, does this constitute normal hospitality, or is it a big deal? In the UK, it is unusual to invite a colleague from abroad home for dinner, but commonplace to go out to the pub for a drink. In South Africa on the other hand, it is commonplace hospitality to invite colleagues from abroad home. If invited, don't forget to take a box of chocolates or some flowers. A bit of research into the customs of the country, ideally through conversations with people who have worked there for years, is good preparation.

Instant returns? Unlikely

There was a neat book published a few years ago called *How to Get a Pay Rise*, by Ros Jay. The memorable advice was: "Be worth it—and know how to ask for it." The same goes for any favour or advancement. The personal and the professional are always closely intertwined. We trust someone we think will do a good job, and our trust grows as they deliver and we come to see them as someone who won't let us down. But if you've gone that extra yard, or mile, and not received the advancement or returned favour you expected, you feel taken for granted and the relationship can turn sour. Stay neutral.

In international settings, these relationships are naturally more complex, and require special attention. Often, more than one form of communication is required to check that there is a shared understanding of expectations. It's helpful to use more than one media: follow up on a meeting with an extra phone call, some texts or emails to update on the progress of a certain project, for example. This is especially the case where one or both of you is communicating in a second language.

> I had a phone call from an ex-colleague after 18 months...
> out of the blue. He had heard I was leaving the country and
> heading home and had phoned to wish me all the best. I was
> touched he still remembered me. An hour later, he sent me
> a text message, asking me to recommend him to my boss,
> for the job I was leaving. I didn't bother to reply. I was so
> disgusted.
>
> —**Marketing manager in a telecoms company in Turkey**

The power of conversations

The deepest, truest relationships come through extended conversations. Creating space for conversations, either face to face or online, is rarely a priority in today's hurried business atmosphere. With the internet operating as a 24/7 worldwide shopping mall, and managers focusing on getting the job done, there is rarely any natural down-time to talk about things other than the task at hand. But it is an essential investment in personal and professional relationships to create this space from time to time.

Thirty or 40 years ago, it was more common for business friends to have long lunches together, where the conversation would roam over a wide range of subjects. Such conversations enable a fuller understanding not just of your partners' skills, aspirations and even immediate worries, but also the deeper motivations that they bring to their work. What were their childhood ambitions? Do they see themselves in a corporate role, or setting up on their own? Is their primary motivation for the current project to earn money and then retire, or is it more about making a reputation for themselves? What *really* matters to someone: the originality of the work, or the attention to detail? Take a moment to think about the last time you had any conversation of this nature, with a colleague, or vendor, or customer. Or even your cousin, neighbour or school friend?

Everyone brings with them to their work a "hinterland"—a phrase coined by the British politician, Denis Healey. This refers to their other interests and their deeper motivations, outside work. For long-term, in-depth relationships, where the outcome is of great importance to at least one of you, it's well worth the while to get to know one another beyond a working relationship, which might be more superficial.

So take the time to find out personal stuff—where you grew up, hobbies and special interests, previous jobs, kids and so on. Bonds often develop from a common passion, whether cricket, football, classical music, dance or hiking. Also, there may be a clue in someone's hinterland why a particular project means so much to him or her. It's the same individual at work as at home, after all.

In a recent offsite, the facilitator insisted we take the time to find out about our colleagues. In the beginning we were all cynical, as we had been working together for the best part of 15 years. We perceived the exercise to be a waste of valuable time. An hour later, however, we were all rather stupefied to learn how little we knew about one another's families, their wives, parents and children, what they did in their spare time, and any hobbies or special interests they had. One guy sang in

a choir, another loved cooking, and one spent four hours every week
volunteering in a children's hospital. Strange how little you can know
about the people with whom you are in regular contact.

— Executive committee member of a
retail business, at a top-team offsite

A more level playing field

There are many challenges and difficulties in beginning to work
globally, and there are many opportunities and rewards. The prospect
of working in a different culture and jurisdiction, with people from
very different backgrounds, feels like it's only a question of challenge
and difficulty. For some, though, it actually can make working life
easier, more interesting and more fun.

Think about some of the challenges people face: gender and
age discrimination, and national and cultural prejudices. In every
country, including those where campaigners and politicians have
gone to great lengths to make matters fairer, there's an unwritten
hierarchy, with a near infinite number of subtle "gradings" indicating
status. When we work in the country of our birth and upbringing,
we are subject to the attitudes that underlie this. The school or
university you went to, your religion, your dining preferences, the
common phrases you use and—above all—the accent you speak
with, often place you somewhere on that hierarchy. Even your
surname can denote low or high status in some regions. In the
Americas, for example, possessing a native American surname has
often been less advantageous than a European one.

When working in the country we grew up in, however we may try to ignore national preferences and stereotypes, it's difficult. How often have you tried not to assume that someone with the manners and voice traditionally associated with a group known for its wealth, influence and emphasis upon educational standards "must" be more intelligent and capable than someone without? Ironically, some people with "progressive" liberal politics are the worst offenders, being dismissive of those from poorer, rural regions associated with conservative views.

In many countries, accent is a major indicator, and for some, the biggest handicap. Generally speaking, "posh" accents, associated with influence and access to the most prestigious educational institutes, urban and middle to upper ranking in class, have the higher status. Accents of the poorer, rural areas have the lowest. Just take a walk around the banking centres in the City of London, and tune your ear to the number of Oxbridge accents!

When working globally, however, this is often less relevant. If you're working with no one from your home country, it may not matter at all. This can be liberating. Your colleagues probably do not know that the accent with which you speak is derived is from an "unfashionable" part of your home country. They do not know that your family could not afford a top university. They do not know that you had to learn English on top of your other studies in the evenings as you held down a day job. As long as you can do your work to a high standard, they will take it that your education is good enough, and they will appreciate the work ethic you are likely to possess if you have come through this route.

Being a Muslim in India made it difficult to get promoted in the Indian company I worked for. In France, no one knew what religion I was; all they knew was that I was from India, and that was enough.

—CFO of a FMCG (fast-moving consumer goods) company,
born in Bangalore and now based in Marseilles

In the global working world, you can get access to people of influence, and work alongside them. In your own country, even if so-called political correctness exists, you might be unequivocally barred from connecting with them. Another possibility is that, when working in our home country, we hold ourselves back with our own feeling of inferiority, for example, that you are from the "wrong side of the street" or a minority religion. The fact that your father was a street cleaner or owned a mom-and-pop store may be a real obstacle in a company where typically fathers were doctors or lawyers. This might form our own worldview—making an assumption we can't progress.

My husband was from a working-class family in the north of England. His accent was a clear giveaway in the bank he worked for in the City of London. That promotion just never came. Strange how quickly he rose to the top when we relocated to Singapore. Within no time he became the Area Head. It was even more surprising to see how our social standing was elevated. We were invited to all sorts of events we would never have made it to in either Manchester or London. For his career, it was the best decision we ever made.

—Wife of Chief Information Officer (Asia) of a British bank

So, for all the difficulties and unexpected prejudices you may still come across when working internationally, for some people it's a more level playing field. You can progress based on your own ability and capacity to learn. You can establish yourself with the confidence and the freedom that flows from this. For some people, the personal profile can grow and flourish more on a global field than within the confines, restrictions and prejudices of the national one. Make the most of it!

We're all publishers now

Just over a decade ago, Tom Peters, in his influential *Fast Company* article, "The Brand Called You," introduced the concept of being the CEO of Me Inc.

> *Regardless of age, regardless of position, regardless of the business we happen to be in, all of us need to understand the importance of branding. We are CEOs of our own companies: Me Inc. To be in business today, our most important job is to be head marketer for the brand called You.*

Some will take to the marketing language more readily than others; all that really underlies it is a simple concept. What is the image, and what are the feelings, that your name evokes in the minds of others? It's worth thinking about that for a while. In the last chapter we discussed developing and nurturing the network—and visualizing it. It's worth also considering how people on that network feel about you.

If you imagine yourself as a mini-enterprise, you can think in terms of short-term earnings, longer term investments and so on. All of these are underpinned by your personal brand. Who are you? How do you come across? Is your reputation deserved? Do you need to do more to promote yourself? Or do you need to do less promotion and spend time to perfect your delivery and have some real success behind you?

It is essential, as a global worker, to have a strong web profile, to be on at least two networking sites, and to have some kind of blog or update. Think about what personal profile you wish for you—and why.

Some people will need a more public profile than others, depending on their role. Marketers, spokespeople, communicators and columnists have the greatest need for a public profile; whereas for some advisers and consultants, their clients may not wish them to be too visible. You need to have the right sort of profile, not necessarily the biggest. Everyone needs a strong network, but some have to be more discreet than others.

A web presence is only a part of developing your personal profile, but it's a key part. The howls of anguish from traditional publishing groups over their declining advertising rates reflect the fact that "we're all publishers now." It takes five minutes to set up a Wordpress blog and begin typing, and a further few minutes to create a customized background. It costs nothing. You could also easily choose some people whom you admire, read their blogs and start communicating with them. Did you ever dream it would be so easy?

Put yourself at the helm

There's a lot of chat and speculation about the web or globalization changing the way we think, behave, and importantly, the way we work. Sometimes, it's as if these are strange forces operating out of our control, and we are just helpless victims. Of course, there are many things we can't do much about; but that makes it all the more important to control the things that we *can*; to remember at all times that we are conscious beings, with free will and the power to chart our own destiny.

Think sailing strategy: You cannot determine the weather, but you can decide if you want to just end up where the wind pushes you, or if you want to trim the sails and set the tiller and plot your own course. It's a lot like that when building your international profile. Use the web, don't let it use you. Control your own career, image and reputation.

This sounds corny to some of you shy wallflowers, but do try to make yourself visible. Volunteer for extra projects, work for an NGO, teach at your local or overseas college, volunteer to be a mentor or to be a trustee for the pension fund. Don't turn down opportunities to be a speaker or be on a panel at conferences, or speak up at a workshop. Never forget to pay attention to and help your colleagues all the time.

Don't become spam

When raising your profile, more is definitely not always best. If you bombard people with messages and self-promotion, you will quickly annoy rather than engage them. Such simplistic, "hard sell" promotion of yourself as a "brand" may have worked in mass-communication advertising in the 20th century, such as for selling soap powder in the early days of television, but is hopelessly ill-equipped for the sophisticated matter of maintaining and promoting yourself in the modern economy. A news presenter at CNN recalls:

One of the people I was friendly with at school is always sending out web links, as to how successful he is. Whenever he gets a promotion or moves jobs he does a mass emailing of the internal announcement in the company. Otherwise, I never hear from him, and he doesn't bother to return emails. I find that nauseating.

EXERCISES
RAISING YOU GLOBAL PROFILE

1. Table the people with whom you are regularly interacting, how often you engage with each of them, and which media you are using (email, social networking, blogging, phone, face-to-face, VC). Highlight the five who play the most important part in your career.

2. Pick three people whose blogs you would like to follow, and join in the comment. They could be academics, politicians, scientists or economists whose views you admire.

3. Make sure you always have your one-minute elevator speech ready and up to date. Write it down and rehearse it. You never know when you might need it.

4. Join Twitter or a social networking site that you think will broaden not only your personal networks, but also your horizons.

5. Improve the search engine ranking of your websites by building cross-links from your pages on sites such as Twitter and Facebook.

continued >>>

6. Build your personal profile. To be successful, anywhere, you will need a strong online profile. Remember to keep it global and free of cultural jargon.

   • A good place to start is at www.google.com/profiles. This link will assist you to understand how to go about it and gives a couple of examples of personal profiles as well

   • Remember that when people choose to click on your name or your photo, they are looking to find out about you—what your expertise is, and what it is your business does. You typically want to include what informs your perspective and opinions and sometimes even hobbies and background. This information should be quick and easy to find on your profile.

   • Choose a photo that best represents you in the context of your role and your business. Make sure that it does not make you seem unfriendly or unapproachable, since the point of being here is to make new contacts.

YOUR ONLINE PROFILE
(SAMPLE)

Hi, I am Alex Smidt, and I am a Virtual Assistant. I have my CVA designation from the International Virtual Assistants Association (www.ivaa.org).

My expertise is in Technical Writing—I supervised the production of manuals for an engineering firm in Frankfurt. I have an MSc in Engineering, and continue to study communication methodologies. Currently, I am writing up the content for web-based eLearning courses, as well as webinar content for the head of operations in that organization.

Prior to becoming an independent consultant/ administrator, I worked in the R&D department of Siemens.

Currently, I am looking for new clients, and welcome the opportunity to service technical information. References can be provided on request.

10 MANAGE YOUR TIME ACROSS TIME ZONES

"If only I had more time," we often find ourselves thinking. When time zones, cultural differences and language complexities are additional ingredients—as you will find in an international role—juggling your time to focus on what really needs to be done requires even more planning and concentration. To stay on top of things, remember that just as we don't have to let technology control us, it's the same with the ticking clock—we can control many aspects of a busy life, with its competing demands and priorities. So, rather than bewailing our inability to slow the spinning of the globe, it's better to look at the matters which can be brought under our jurisdiction:

Setting priorities: Does everything have to be done now; this minute; tomorrow? What are the real deadlines in the eyes of the customers and other key stakeholders? If I can't attend to something straight away, I need to plan when I will do it, set reminders to make sure I do, and communicate with the people waiting for my input so that expectations are understood. In a global role, you might have the luxury of solving a problem or deliberating over a decision while a person on the other side of the world is fast asleep. On the other hand, you may need to complete an assignment before you leave for home, so that your customer or boss has what he or she needs, no matter how late it is for you.

Managing relationships: All reasonable people in your network know that you have other commitments and cannot attend to their needs exclusively, 24/7. Dealing with clashing, or competing deadlines or events means handling relationships sensitively. If you cannot attend to something, or be somewhere, you need to think about how that affects the relationship—and check back with the person when you can. But at least take the time to connect with them and let them know how you stand.

Effective delegation: If you are a key member of an international team, it will help your colleagues, bosses and customers to know who they might contact if you are unavailable. Make sure you set up your "out of office" reply on your emails, leaving the contact details of one or more of your team members so that people are aware as to why you are not responding, and to whom they may turn for assistance. This also helps to ensure your colleagues have realistic expectations of your availability and when you might respond. Consider the following anecdote:

> *I now refuse to carry a Blackberry, as it almost broke up my marriage. I would get up at 3 a.m. to go to the bathroom and land up checking my emails sometimes for as long as half an hour. Finally, thank goodness, my wife put her foot down. But by then every one of my team members had gotten used to the idea that I would answer emails within a couple of hours no matter which time zone I was in. She finally refused to have it in the house, as I was unable to stop checking the gadget every few minutes.*

> — London-based manager of an outsourcing division of an Indian company, with teams in North Carolina, Chennai, Dublin, Krakow and Melbourne

Sound familiar? How many of you sometimes end up in bed with your laptop, especially if your partner or spouse does too? How many of you have juggled a crying baby on your knee while typing with one finger? The stress of getting through work across time zones can indeed be completely overwhelming, especially if you let it take over your life.

Managing one's time is difficult enough at the best of times, but managing one's time across time zones adds a whole new dimension to getting work done in what was once considered a normal 40–50-hour work week. When travel also invades your space, you might

---

TIME MANAGEMENT BASICS

Many of you have read about, or had a training programme on time management. If you are not familiar with the basics, you can find numerous e-learning programs, articles and links on the subject. Here are some to get you going:

- *Time Management* by Randy Pausch:
  video.google.com/videoplay?docid=-5784740380335567758

- Woopidoo.com: www.woopidoo.com

- Email Overload Training Experts: www.getcontrol.net

- MindTools Time Management Training:
  www.mindtools.com/pages/main/newMN_HTE.htm

well find yourself getting home after everyone has gone to bed, and flying out to meetings on your weekend. Those work weeks can stretch well past 55 hours. If you are always checking your emails late at night and early morning, before you realize it there is not much time for anything else.

The best place to start is with you

At the beginning of your next work week, table to the quarter-hour how much time you are actively spending on work. This does not necessarily mean the time you think about work while driving, or walking to the train. Rather it is best to only include time on the phone, time writing and answering emails, time on conference calls and VCs, time in meetings and time actually working on particular assignments. If you are working from home in the mornings and evenings, don't forget to include this as well. You might be surprised as to how your work life has submerged the rest of your life.

Next, make a plan of how much time you wish to spend doing what and where. It is fine to take calls in the evening and catch up on emails before you get to the office; just become aware of what you are doing and when. Importantly, take control of your time.

The Chinese company that I work for is based just out of Beijing, and operates 24 hours a day, 7 days a week. Some of our vendors are based in India and Georgia, and it is an ongoing struggle to ensure we have the right inventory to manufacture our products. Usually, I am struggling to make sure we have enough raw material available. Supplies often get stuck in ports, and customs issues can be

*troublesome, and often need to be sorted with great urgency. I seem
to be on call 24/7. Although I have a competent team, I am reluctant
to ask them to be on call to give me some time off, as they are also
very busy.*

— Chang W., procurement manager
for a car manufacturing company

On reflection, working on the above exercise, Chang came
to realize it was not necessarily he himself who needed to be on
constant call. After all, he did have a perfectly competent team.
"Why," he asked himself, "did he have this need to know and be
in control of everything?" He began to plan the work in a more
organized fashion, and create clear accountabilities in his team as
to who did what and when. Within a few months of learning to let
go and empower his team, he found he was able to take up fencing
again—a sport he loved and that kept him fit. He reflected:

*It is strange how I didn't even realize what lovely parts of my life
had disappeared. I had imagined that I, and only I, was capable
of doing some of the work. Strange now to acknowledge how that
happened, and that with a bit of forethought and planning I took
control again.*

And, by the way, his team felt as if at last they were learning
new things, and enjoyed stepping up to take more responsibility.

Each of us has many large priorities in our life, such as pursuing
a particular career path, buying a home, or setting up a business. We

also have things we really enjoy doing. To top it off, there are things we have to do, like shopping, the dishes, family commitments. Be careful of the many things that simply clutter up your time. Take some time to reflect on three things truly close to your heart. They could range from keeping fit, your job, a special hobby, meeting friends, to spending real quality time with the kids.

Routine tasks, odd times

If you work in an international team, or are a member of multiple teams, or travel frequently—or any combination of the above— you'll need to invent unusual times and locations to catch up. You may have a tele-conference at nine in the evening, and catch up with personal matters the next morning. You write a presentation while in the airport departure lounge; read a paper spread out on the breakfast bar while the coffee is brewing; make an important call on the mobile on the way to the dry cleaners. You may mull over a work problem while going for a run or engaging in some routine chores, like cooking, shaving, or washing the dishes. When you wake up jetlagged at four in the morning, you can decide whether to do some yoga, unpack your suitcase or finish that report.

Inspiration can come from the unlikeliest sources, at the unlikeliest times. Famously, Shell's innovative "bendy straw drill," used for extracting difficult-to-reach oil while minimizing environmental disruption, was inspired by engineer Jaap van Ballegooijen's noticing, while taking his son for a burger and a drink, how the boy inverted the kinked straw to access bits of milkshake that were stuck underneath the ice cubes.

Having said all this, it's valuable to have some time completely switched-off from work; to let the brain lie fallow and recuperate; to let your personal relationships have time and space, un-squeezed by work thoughts and demands. We wouldn't drive our cars or our PCs into the ground, without servicing or repair; we owe much more to ourselves and our families.

Manage expectations

A good place to start dealing with the dreaded overwhelming feeling of "too much to do and never enough time in the day to do it" is a good old-fashioned "To Do" list. But don't just put down what needs to be done; more importantly, put down how you're going to make time for the important people in your life. Effective time management is as much about managing relationships as managing hours and minutes, that quality time that you spend with colleagues, family, friends and customers… really being there for them.

Think about the people whom you would wish to respond to immediately, or stay in touch with regularly, even a couple of times during the day. Decide whom the most important calls and emails are from: my husband; my boss, or bosses; my kids; my customers; my team; my parents; my friends; the ever-important nanny.

Which of these people are the most important will vary, naturally, from week to week, and from day to day, as deadlines, work pressures, demands and unscheduled events such as illnesses have their impact.

Prepare separate folders in your email program. That way, you are not faced with hundreds of emails daily in a disorganized fashion, but are clear about the emails you need to deal with promptly. If there are particular family members or friends that you would like instant connection with, the instant-messaging application on your mobile phone can let you know straight away. Set different ring tones on your mobile phone to help you decide which calls to take, and which ones to leave "for now."

If you are a team leader, do let your team know if there are any particular times (over the weekend or in the evenings) which are not convenient for you to take calls. Text messages are a great way to send or receive messages in an unobtrusive way. Make it work for you.

Make your own PSLAs

If you are on the road a lot, it is often useful to make some "personal service level agreements" (PSLAs) with the folks at home and in the workplace, in which you define the level of "service" that they can expect from you:

> *My wife knows that I always call when my flight has landed, no matter what time. The kids know that I will phone them every night around half an hour before they go to sleep. Sometimes it is hard for me to phone at those times, but I make it a point of never missing it, even if it is 3 a.m. in my world.*
>
> —Head of Sales for a global car maker, based in Tokyo

You might also wish to decide that, unless flying, you typically respond to emails from your boss within an hour or two, colleagues in different locations within four hours, and customers within two hours. Importantly, get back to people as soon as you can and let them know that you have received their email and when you might respond more fully, if it is something you need to either think about or investigate. It is difficult to connect if they do not receive a response they were waiting for after a day, and are left wondering if their email was read, ignored, or considered unimportant. Be careful you don't get the nickname of "I will get back to you," if you typically just use it as an ongoing stalling tactic.

Wake up, it is time to go to sleep

If you travel a lot for work, jet lag is something that will continue to harass you, no matter what you do to avoid it. Some people find medication works, but it is best to seek a doctor's advice. If you follow the basic pointers—avoid alcohol, tea and coffee, and drink lots of water to keep hydrated—you should be able to deal with it. Keep fit and walk pre- and post-flight. In the airport, walk around; most city hubs are big enough to give you 20 minutes around the terminal if you are in transit or early for your flight.

Explain to your families, who perhaps do not travel across time zones, how jet lag affects you. Then they won't worry if they see you dozing off at strange times or struggling with insomnia when you should be sleeping.

EXERCISE
WORLD TIME AWARENESS

Early in this book, we recommended the exercise of looking at the world from an unfamiliar point on the globe. That simple mental exercise helps us maintain the awareness that the company and the worker are linked to the world, and the world is a globe.

Awareness of time differences is closely linked to this— as is the awareness of time. The world economy ticks 24/7, but that doesn't mean that you have to.

1. Make a list of the countries, and towns within those countries, where you have customers, vendors, colleagues, bosses, family and friends. Then table the time difference as a plus or minus from where you are. For example, if you are working for an NGO and based in Kabul, and your HQ is in Houston (-9.30), your funding comes from Brussels (-2.30), and your parents live in Melbourne (+5.30), you can have a ready reckoner on hand.

2. For some countries, mainly those in the West, the weekend is Saturday and Sunday. For many in the Middle East, it is Friday and Saturday or only Friday. For some only Saturday. Make a list of those

continued >>>

countries where you work and connect with at a personal level, to ensure you do not bother people on their day off.

3. Remember that many countries have daylight saving time and switch backwards and forwards in the fall and spring. Check the dates that this change happens; it does vary between North America and Europe.

4. Make a note of the various office hours that people tend to keep in different locations. In Mumbai, for example, offices open officially at 10 a.m., but people might arrive anytime between 10 and 11 a.m. and leave between 6 and 7.30 p.m. Contrast that to New York, where people are at their desks mostly from 8 a.m. but home by 5.30 p.m. to have dinner with their kids. European hours do not differ much; only Scandinavian countries tend to start work much earlier than other countries.

5. Make "The World Clock: Time Zone Converter" a bookmark page. You will be able to find out the right time in the location you wish in a second (www. timeanddate.com/worldclock/converter.html).

CONCLUSION
SET THE SAIL TO CATCH THE GLOBAL WIND

As we continue to move towards a world economy that is more integrated, hundreds of millions of people will be required to be operating globally. At the same time, it is neither desirable nor possible for the histories, institutions, cultures and culinary tastes of the different nations around the world to be merged into a single homogenized whole. There will always be opposition towards perceived domineering multi-national enterprises, offshoring, migration and loss of certain ways of life. But friendship knows no boundaries; and where friendships and partnerships flourish, there will be business. There is even speculation that Facebook could become a bank!

Take a moment to consider how many different nationalities were in the last spaceship: a global team of thirteen Americans, three Russians, one Ukrainian, and one Israeli—that would have been unthinkable in the early 90s. It is worthy of note that until 2003, astronauts were sponsored and trained exclusively by governments, either by the military, or by civilian space agencies. However, with the sub-orbital flight of the privately-funded SpaceShipOne in 2004, a new category of astronaut was created: the commercial astronaut. These space travellers could be from anywhere.

We are also starting to see very high levels of international collaboration, with cross-border solutions, as environmental pressures continue to be felt with a growing human population.

An increasing number of people in the world are of mixed lineage and identity—their parents are from different countries, they have often moved location as children, and they are likely to have studied and worked in more than one country. You could imagine, say, someone with a Kenyan father and a white American mother, attending school in Hawaii and Indonesia, going on to become President of the United States of America. Though that does sound a little far-fetched.

At an institutional level, the credit crisis showed the influence that the nation-state continues to wield, but also illustrated its limitations. More people are engaging and trading with one another than ever before. Hopefully, cross-country partnerships and business opportunities will continue to contribute to open debate on the environment, nuclear activities, mutual support in times of natural disasters, economic crises, and of course, peace.

Even the most basic functions of the web have fundamentally altered perspectives. Twenty years ago, if you wanted to read the newspaper of a different country, you had to take out an expensive subscription, or locate yourself in a capital city where the larger newsagents and bookshops would have overseas publications. Now you can just look online, and most of the content is free. If you wanted to make new relationships with people in different regions and practise your language skills, there was no alternative but to travel. Now you can do so through LinkedIn, Twitter, the World Café, Facebook and so on. There's greater need to think and operate globally, develop a cross-cultural mindset, and more opportunity to do so. This makes being a Global You considerably easier.

It remains a formidable personal challenge, of course. Barriers to global working are practical as well as cultural: learning languages, dealing with time differences, keeping up to date with technology, coping with jet lag, balancing work and family responsibilities. Overcoming cultural differences and prejudices still remains complex, but no longer overwhelmingly so, as people travel more and more frequently for work and for fun.

And in spite of the challenges of global thinking and working there is a huge groundswell, all over the world, of goodwill, strong business sense, and the desire to connect or trade with people on the other side of the world. And there's a huge desire to learn how. What's more, this feeling exists in all countries, rich and poor, Western and Eastern. News media inevitably concentrate on crisis, division and conflict, creating negative images about some regions and countries. Under the surface, though, most "ordinary" people just want a good job, good career opportunities, and good prospects for their family. If these are not around on home territory, then why not work abroad? These natural aspirations are coming within reach of many people in previously so-called under-developed regions, as the rise of the BRIC countries—Brazil, Russia, India and China—shows.

This has huge implications for international companies, who are adjusting to seeing such regions as consumer bases as well as manufacturing locations. Cultural learning and diversification of thinking are today a must for the Western-based consumer goods companies, every bit as much as for the rising technology firms of India.

Implement these ten strategies in *The Global You* and you will be well-equipped to be a strong global player. There are no shortcuts. Keep Preparing, keep on Practising and always Plan. We look forward to bumping into you somewhere, sometime, in the global village. You can follow our blog at humaninternet.wordpress.com, and follow us on Twitter, @felipewh or @monsue8.

BIBLIOGRAPHY

Aditya Birla Group, Gyanodaya. "How Global are You." 2010. http://www.adityabirla.com/careers/gyanodaya.asp.

Adler, N.J. "Conclusion: Future Issues in Global Leadership Development." In M.E. Mendenhall, T.M. Kühlman & G.K. Stahl (eds), *Developing Global Leaders: Policies, Processes, and Innovations*. Westport, CT: Quorum Books, 2001.

Black, J.S., H.B. Gregersen, M.E. Mendenhall, & J. McNett. *Globalizing People Through International Assignments*. New York: Addison-Wesley Longman, 1999.

Broad, L.M. & W.J. Newstrom. *Transfer of Training*. New York: Addison-Wesley, 1992.

Davis, D.D. & J.L. Bryant. "Influence at a Distance: Leadership in Global Virtual Teams." In W.H Mobley & P.W. Dorfman (eds), *Advances in Global Leadership* (Vol. 3). Stamford, CT: JAI Press, 2003.

Dorfman, P.W. "Introduction." In W.H Mobley & P.W. Dorfman (eds), *Advances in Global Leadership* (Vol 3). Stamford, CT: JAI Press, 2003.

Garavaglia, P. "Transfer of Training" in *American Society for Training and Development*, No. 9512. Alexandria, VA: American Society for Training and Development, 1955.

Georgenson, D.L. "The Problem of Transfer Calls for Partnership" in *Training and Development Journal*, 36 (10), 1982.

Georges, J.C. "The Myths of Soft-skills Training" in *Training*, 33 (1), p. 48, 1996.

Goleman, D. *Social Intelligence*. New York: Bantam Dell, 2007.

Goodwin, Doris Kearns. *Team of Rivals*. New York: Simon & Schuster, 2005.

Gupta, A.K. & V. Govindarajan. "Cultivating a Global Mind-set" in *Academy of Management Executive*, Vol. 16, No. 1, pp. 116-125, 2002.

Hessler, P. *Oracle Bones*. New York: Harper Collins, 2006.

Hoffmann, Charlotte. *An Introduction to Bilingualism*. London: Longman, 1991.

Jeannet, J.P. *Managing with a Global Mindset*. Financial Times/ Prentice Hall, 2000.

Joni, S.-N. & D. Beyer. "How to Pick a Good Fight" in *Harvard Business Review*, December 2009.

Klein, Joe. "Obama's Team of Rivals" in *Time*, 18 June 2008.

McCall, M.W. & G.P. Hollenbeck. *Developing Global Executives*. Boston: Harvard Business School Press, 2002.

McGilchrist, Iain. *The Master and His Emissary: The Divided Brain and the Making of the Western World*. New Haven: Yale University Press, 2009.

Midgley, Mary. "The Master and His Emissary" *Guardian* review, 2 January 2010.

Mohan, A. *Making Learning Stick*. Gyanodaya, Aditya Birla Group, 2009.

Paris, Kathleen A. *The Clover Practice: Staying Healthy in Sick Organisations*. Charleston: BookSurge, 2008.

Pink, Daniel. *A Whole New Mind*. London: Marshall Cavendish, 2008.

Schneider, S., & J.L. Barsoux. *Managing Across Cultures*. London: Financial Times/Prentice Hall, 2003.

Senge, Peter, et al. *Schools That Learn*. New York: Doubleday, 2001.

Sobel, Dava. *Longitude: The True Story of a Lone Genius Who Solved the Greatest Scientific Problem of His Time*. New York: Walker, 1995.

Subedi, B.S. "Emerging Trends on Transfer of Learning" in *International Education Journal*, Vol. 5, No. 4, 2004.

Vinkenburg, C.J., P.G.W. Jansen & W. den Dekker. *Dimensions of an Individual Global Mindset*. http://ideas.repec.org/p/dgr/vuarem/2005-14.html.

ACKNOWLEDGEMENTS

Over the past few years we have carefully listened to many CEOs, senior managers, and employees at all levels. It is their insights, knowledge and experiences which have built the foundation of this book. They have shared successes and failures, passions and anxieties, and of course many practical and useful ideas about multi-continent and multi-cultural working. We are most grateful for their time and views. These challenges impact all generations from rookies to top teams and gurus, from everywhere and anywhere, and we are confident that those learning experiences will be useful and interesting to all readers.

To the hundreds of managers on all continents, who took the time to complete the online questionnaire, it is thanks to them all that we were able to ground this book firmly into research.

The team at Gyanodaya, the Aditya Birla Institute of Management Learning, provided valuable support into the study of global managers, and we are grateful for their assistance.

We also thank the children of family and friends, who appear to be so much more confident and comfortable with technology and global knowledge. We all have much to learn from their very different worldviews.

To Martin Liu and Justin Lau at Marshall Cavendish, many thanks for your ongoing support, advice and feedback.

ABOUT THE AUTHORS
SUSAN BLOCH

Susan Bloch recently spent three-and-a-half years working for two global Indian conglomerates, and is now working as an executive coach and leadership consultant in Seattle, USA. She has coached top teams in many of the FTSE100 and Fortune500 companies across the globe over the past 20 years. A truly global citizen, she has lived and worked in five countries—South Africa, the USA, Israel, the UK, and India—and worked extensively in Europe. Before moving to India, she was partner and Head of Thought Leadership at Whitehead Mann in London, operating as an executive coach, and conducting board effectiveness reviews. A Chartered Psychologist, Susan has co-authored *How to Manage in a Flat World* (published in eight languages), *Employability*, and *Complete Leadership*, and has produced a number of research publications.

PHILIP WHITELEY

Philip Whiteley is an author and journalist, specializing in management, particularly the areas of leadership, motivation and strategic human resources. He has written numerous articles for *The Times*, where he contributed a weekly column on strategic reward; for *Personnel Today*, *Director*, *CorpComms*, *Employee Benefits*, and many other titles; and has appeared on BBC Newsnight discussing the portrayal of the workplace in the media. He is the author or co-author of eight books and major reports. The focus of his work is to challenge the mechanistic approach of much business theory, drawing on evidence that shows that a humanistic approach is more profitable. He is chair of the Human Capital Forum, and editor-in-chief of *Payroll World*. He has given numerous conference speeches. He is a member of the Society of Authors, and a Subject Matter Expert for the Chartered Management Institute.